The Iceland Bus

by

Edward Conduit

&

Jean Scott-Smith

Norse names in the Central Lakes

Over 1200 years ago small ships braved the North Atlantic between Iceland and the British Isles. Some of these ships brought settlers to North-West England, the area we now call Cumbria. We still know their names for the landscape and Lakeland famers still use some of their words for their animals. They were one the many Norse emigrant communities, which were amazingly widely-spread: they reached America, Constantinople and even Baghdad. Movement was not all one way: genetic analysis shows that many early Icelandic women were from the British Isles. The old ethnic connections came to have new significance during the dark days of World War Two. Fishing boats carried intelligence and agents between the Shetlands and Norway, under the noses of the Nazis. The brave Norsemen of this "Shetland bus" are our inspiration in exploring that other historical connection, between Iceland and Cumbria. We shall call it The Iceland Bus.

The cover picture shows how sheep husbandry provides the greatest continuity between Lakeland dialect and old Danish. A **wether** is a castrated male sheep Isl: *vedhr*. A **hogget** or hogg is a young (9 to 18 months) sheep of either sex; Isl *hakkað*. An *aera* is a ewe, though aira force waterfall could also be from either ON *eyrr*, a gravel bank and *á*, river. **Gimmer** is a particular peak, and in Icelandic *gimbur* - a female sheep. The saga author Snorri Sturluson had another *gimmer* - 'be-gemmed', a level of heaven. **Lug**: this sheep ear marking is possibly Isl *lög merkja* - law mark - or Nynorsk *lugge*; but lug is also slang for ear in Northern English and Scots. **Smit** is a sheep coat mark using coloured grease; it may be the past tense of Isl *að smjör*.

The most interesting similarity is rigg welter. This describes a sheep falling on its back, sometimes with tetanus. Because of this knockout effect, it has been used to show the strength of a particular beer. It turns out that the phrase *rigg velta* means "on the back, fall" in modern West Norse. The fjords of Western Norway are the most likely original source for migrants to both Cumbria and Iceland, though the Isle of Man may have been a "bus stop" on the way. We shall be tracing their progress later in this book.

A virtual walk up Langdale reveals how West Norse settlers named the places they encountered. The Brathay ('broad', 'river') meets the Rothay ('red', 'river') south west of Ambleside. The name of the town suggests they found an *á* ('river') with a *melr* ('sand bank'), where they erected a *sætr* ('shieling'), a hut for summer use with flocks. Carrying on you pass hamlets named from features of the river: Clappersgate ('stones thrown down', 'road') and Skelwith ('resounding', 'ford'). Loughrigg ('leek-growing', 'ridge') is the higher ground to the north. The river widens out into Elterwater ('swan', 'lake') get higher in Great Langdale Beck ('long', 'valley', 'stream'). The westbound road stops at Dungeon Ghyll ('ravine'), but you can climb to Stickle Tarn ('prickle/ steep', 'teardrop') or Mickleden ('large', 'Danish'). Now read on!

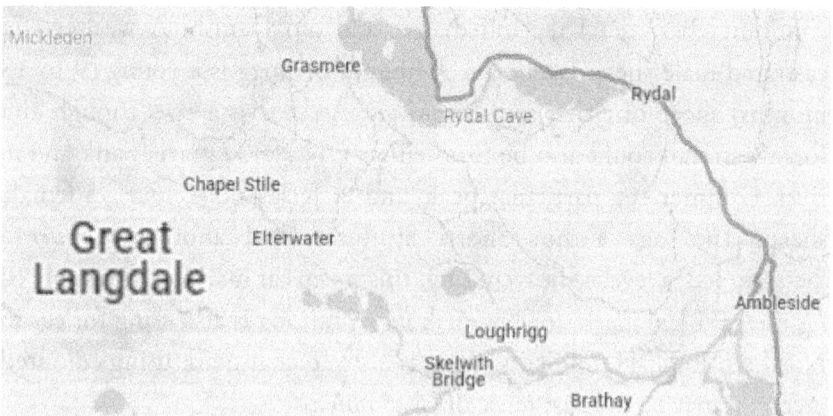

Britons Retreat

The people of the British Isles at the time of the Roman conquest may be considered loosely as Celts. They spoke related languages of Irish Gaelic, Pictish, Welsh and Cumbric. The last of these was spoken in "The Old North" (*yr hen ogledd*), which stretched from the Mersey to the Clyde and joined Wales. One of the largest Cumbric kingdoms was Rheged. Its most famous leader is king Urien, who is said to have had his home in Lywyfenedd (probably the area of the Lyvennet River in Westmorland). Urien's name is preserved in the name of the hill fort known as Castle Hewin, whilst nearby is Tarn Wadling (the second part deriving from the word Gwyddelan, an Irish saint). There is a further myth that Dunmail, "the last king of Cumberland" is buried at Dunmail Raise, though this follows a battle in 945.

After the Romans retreated some Celtic communities attempted to preserve Roman culture, so that Welsh contains borrowings from Latin, such as "ffenster" and "eglwys" that do not occur in English. The legend of King Arthur and the Welsh dragon are legacies of this time. The knights of the round table might be seen as a nostalgic attempt to maintain the tradition of high-status cavalrymen. The dragon may actually come from a windsock carried by horse archers to correct their aim; if so, the Welsh dragon and the knights were actually mercenaries from near the Caspian Sea!

The history of *yr hen ogledd* in these times from a Welsh standpoint is recorded in the works of its famous poet Taliesin. Although he died around 599 CE, texts attributed to him were named the Book of Taliesin in the 17th century. Taliesin, whose name is taken from one of his stories meaning "brow-shining", was a bard (or *bardd*) to three Welsh kings, of whom Urien features most strongly in the poems. Urien in 574 laid siege to Lindisfarne then occupied by the Anglians, and won a notable victory at the battle of Catterick. Rheged was finally annexed by Northumbria about AD 730, some years after a Rheged princess married a Northumbrian. The kingdom of Strathclyde continued until about 1150, with its inhabitants presumably speaking Cumbric. The Kingdom of Strathclyde was then incorporated into the Kingdom of Scotland. The Cumbric language probably died out at about the same time.

William Wallace is a curious relic of that history. Although he is a hero of "Scotland" after his role defeating England at the battle of Stirling, he might alternatively be regarded as "Welsh". The surname Wallace sounds the same as "Wallis", which is the word for Wales in both Old English and Modern German. Saxons spoke of the Celts as Wallis. This name, as well as "Wales" and "Welsh" are traced to the Proto-Germanic word "Walhaz" meaning "foreigner", "stranger". Then it was used by the Germanic peoples to describe inhabitants of the former Roman Empire, who remained Romanised and spoke Latin or Celtic languages. The same etymological origin is shared by the names of various other Celtic or Latin peoples such as the Walloons and the Vlachs, as well as of the Swiss canton of Valais. Meanwhile Celtic speakers used the words Saesneg or Sassenach to describe Saxons. The Scots Gaelic epithet "Sassenach" was copied by speakers of north Northumbrian English of their southern Saxon neighbours.

The people of the British Isles was a major genetic study by the Welcome Foundation published by Callaway,E. (2015). They found people whose four grandparents lived within 10 miles of where they still live. The people of south and east England form a single gene pool, mostly Anglo Saxon but with some Celtic. There about ten genetic groupings in northern England, and perhaps five in modern Wales. Different migrations took place during the Mesolithic and the Neolithic eras, and which laid the foundations for the present-day populations in the British Isles. The Gwynedd group seems to originate from the Iberian Peninsula. According to Stephen Oppenheimer 96% of lineages in Llangefni in north Wales derive from Iberia. The Y-chromosome of Welsh and Irish men shows a large proportion of ancestry with the Basques of Northern Spain and South Western France.

Although Celtic languages were once the language of the British Isles, there is very little trace of Welsh in modern English. Loanwords from Welsh in standard English are only these few: corgi, cwm, cromlech, crag, coracle, flummery, Dad. Penguin, which means 'head, white' may come from Welsh or Cornish. "Flannel" is possibly of Welsh origin. In addition, some English people recognise a few words associated with Welsh culture: eisteddfod, cynghanedd, gorsedd, kistvaen, wrasse, lech, and tref. That is about the extent of the influence of Welsh on English - less than that of Maori or the Incan language Quechua.

While Welsh was still being used in Glasgow as late as 1100, the people of Cumbria perhaps gave up their language when Rheged was annexed by Northumbria around 730 CE. The following words used in the Lakes could be Welsh:

Crag rocks. Either from Brythonic (*craig*) or Goidelic (Gaelic *creag*).

Brat apron. It is found in Welsh ('rag, clout; pinafore'), Scots and N. English dialects but may be an Old English borrowing from Old Irish.

Coble small flat bottomed boat akin to W.*ceubal* "a hollow" and L. *caupulus*; (also N East)

Jannock fair play, just; from Welsh *iawn*, "right, equitable"; though perhaps Norse *jafn*

Joram a large mess from Welsh *goramlu*, "superabundance"; Jack Manning uses this

Vug a fissure in rock, probably came from Cornish mine experts a few centuries ago, but could be Pictish or Gaelic.

The Scottish dialect of English has more loanwords from Welsh, and also Scots Gaelic.

Lum – Scottish word for chimney (Middle Welsh *llumon* "chimney", Gaelic *laom* or *laoman*), as in the saying "lang may yer lum reek"; reek is "smoke", also found in Cumbrian **rowky**

Bach cowpat (cf Welsh *baw* "dung", Gaelic *buadhar*)

Brogat a type of mead (Welsh *bragod* "bragget" – also found in Chaucer)

Baivenjar a mean fellow (Welsh *bawyn* "scoundrel")

Croot a small boy (Welsh *crwt*, Gaelic *cruit* 'small and humpbacked')

Croude type of small harp, as opposed to clarsach (Welsh *crwth* "fiddle", Gaelic *croit*)

Vendace a fish of Derwent Water and Bassenthwaite Lake, cognate with Welsh *gwyniad*

So there are a few more Welsh words in the Lakes and South-West Scotland than there are in standard English. What about grammar? While Scots has some distinct structures such as "I should could wash my car" and "places outwith Scotland", there are not many grammatical innovations in Lakeland speech.

Names of rivers and some hills are the main source for our knowledge of the Cumbric language. Celtic place name elements include *pen* (head), *glen* and *glyn* (valley), *blaen* (top) and *caer* (fortress). These may date from the pre-Roman period, as do some of the river names, **Ehan, Irt, Esk, Mite, Kent, Lune**. The largest survival of Cumbric names are to be found in Cumberland. The old county of Cumberland means 'the land of the Cymry', 'fellow countrymen', as viewed by Saxons in the kingdom of Northumbria. Its neighbour to the south, Westmorland, previously

Westmaringaland, means 'The land of the people of the Western Border'. The modern county of Cumbria also takes its name from *kombrogi*.

Welsh names for hills and rivers are often simply common nouns or adjectives, unlike Saxon names which may include the name of their owner: **Calder** 'rocky, fast flowing river' from Br *caled dubro*; **Cocker** 'crooked river' from Br *kukra* or *crumbaco*; **Dacre** 'trickling stream' from Br *dakru*; **Ehen** probably 'cold river' from a Br word related to Welsh *iain*, 'cold'; **Kent** probably from Br *cunetio* meaning 'sacred one'; **Levens** 'smooth-flowing river' from a Br word related to Welsh *llyfyn*, 'smooth'. **Pen-y-Ghent** in Yorkshire is unchanged from its Welsh roots - pen meaning 'head' or 'hill' and ghent, possibly equivalent to Welsh *caint* or *gwynt*, thus either 'Hill on the Border' or 'Hill of The Winds'. **Torpenhow Hill** combines the languages of all the people that lived here, as each of the four syllables means 'hill'.

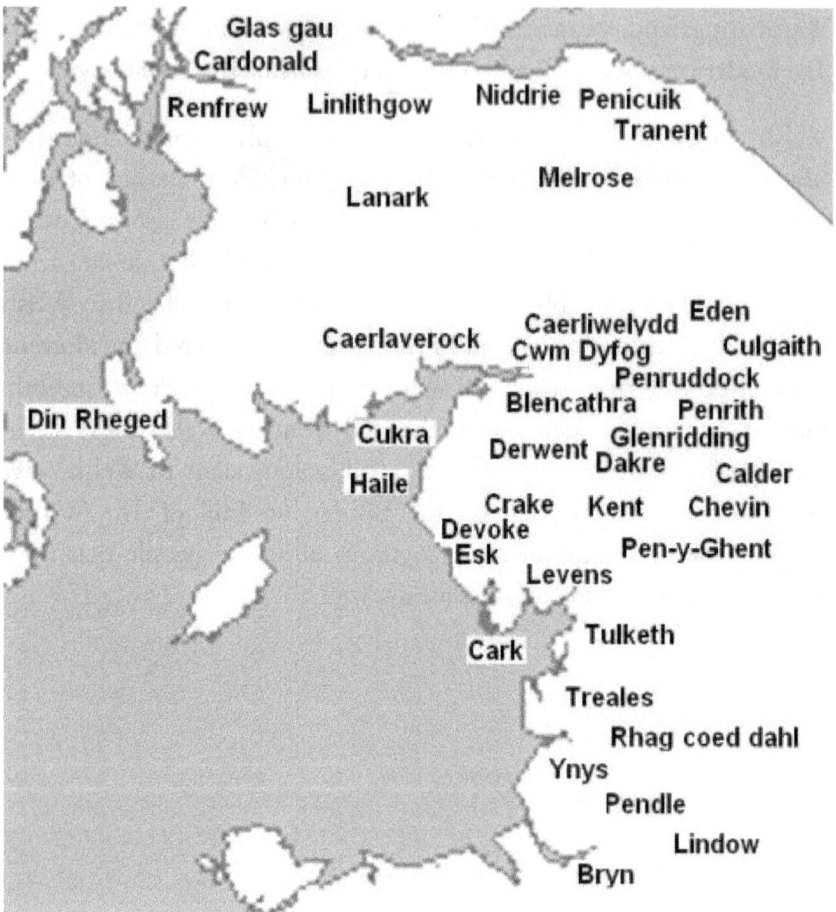

Rheged is thought to have centred on the river Eden, which flows north-west past Penrith towards Carlisle before reaching the Solway Firth. The name Eden itself is closer to Irish Gaelic than Welsh: *edenn* ('ivy'), vs *"eidheann"*. Place names associated with the *cymry* are therefore most numerous west of Penrith and east of Carlisle. **Penrith** itself comes from *pen* ('hill or head') and *rith* (Welsh *rhyd* - a ford). **Penruddock** includes *pen, rudd* (red) and *dokk* (a hollow valley). **Blencathra** contain the word *blaen* (top) and *cadair* (chair or seat). **Blencowe** also uses blaen, but the second element might be *how* - hill, though not in Welsh. **Glencoyne** and **Glenridding** contain the element *glyn* 'valley' with second elements *cawn* ('reed grass') and *rhedyn* ('fern or bracken'). **Catsidicam** (casticam) comes from *catt* ('wild cat', *stig* 'path', *camb* 'ridge'. **Greystoke** is *craik* - crooked and *stak* - stream. **Derwent** water includes the word *derry* ('oaks') or *derwentio* ('abounding in oaks'); this root is also found in Londonderry.

Some Lakeland names sound Welsh, but may not be. **Helvellyn** looks Welsh and has been argued to mean Lauvelln from *helfa* ('hunting ground' + *llyn* ('lake'); however, it may be more modern. **Old Man** of Coniston is probably *allt maen* ('steep place', 'stone') in Welsh, though it might be 'cairn, pile of stones' in Anglo-Saxon. **Greenodd** looks like a Welsh "dd", but is green plus the Norse word *odd* for 'corner'. The Cumbric speech of Rheged and Strathclyde can also be detected further north: Glasgow ('green hollow'), Lanark, Niddrie, Melrose, Renfrew, Tranent, etc. Dun Rhagit near Stranraer was a Rheged fort. Cumbric Christian connections may be found between Cumbrian churches and Glasgow, in the form of dedications to Kertigern, also known as Mungo.

The other persisting feature of Welsh is yan-tan-tether counting. These sheep-counting systems were widely spread in Britain until quite recently. Shepherds in Wiltshire used to use them up to two generations ago and there is a version in Ayrshire. They are now more frequently heard in children's games. The children's rhyme "Hickory-Dickory-Dock, the mouse ran up the clock" is probably also derived from Welsh counting: "hickory" is 8, "dickory" 9, and "dock" is 10. (Opie, 1960). The following list shows the numbers from one to twenty as they are reported from the Coniston fells, and the same number would be said in modern Welsh.

The count normally stops at 20, though Welsh has higher numbers. Scores were counted by the shepherd putting a pebble in his pocket. Five" (pump or pimp) and "ten" (dec or dick) tend to be similar across the Lakes and with Welsh. Twenty (gigget or jiggot) is similar across the fells but not with Welsh. But the less frequently used numbers between six and ten are not very similar across the fells, or like Welsh. "Six" would be Sethera in Borrowdale, Hofa in Eskdale, and Settera in Westmorland. Two other similar features are that yan-tan follows the Welsh pattern of after ten putting the less significant number first, and starting again at fifteen. As Welsh has not been spoken in the Lake District for 1300 years, it is somewhat amazing there is any similarity!

There is a much deeper level of agreement in counting systems. In Urdu, the official language of Pakistan, counting from one to five goes: *aik, do, teen, char, panch*. In Modern Greek it goes: *enas, thio, tris, tesseris, pente*. It turns out that nearly all the languages of Europe and many of South Asia come the same ancient root, called Indo-European. We can still hear our very remote ancestors when people say the numbers one, two, three and ten in their own language in Vladivostok, Kabul or Galway.

Welsh has certainly been pushed into the background in English, almost to the point of extinction. It is only slightly less hard to find Welsh in Lakes dialect and Scots. Yet the evidence of our Celtic ancestors is there if you look hard enough. The same Celtic ancestors reappear in a surprising place - they took the Iceland bus and became the first women colonists of Iceland. We shall look at this in more detail in the chapter "Iceland is born".

1 **Yan** *Un*

2 **Taen** *Dau*

3 **Tedderte** *Tri*

4 **Medderte** *Pedwar*

5 **Pimp** *Pump*

6 **Haata** *Chwech*

7 **Slaata** *Saith*

8 **Lowra** *Wyth*

9 **Dowra** *Naw*

10 **Dick** *Deg*

11 **Yan-a-Dick** *Un ar ddeg*

12 **Taen-a-Dick** *Dau ar ddeg*

13 **Tedder-a-Dick** *Tri ar ddeg*

14 **Medder-a-Dick** *Pedwar ar ddeg*

15 **Mimph** *Pymtheg*

16 **Yan-a-Mimph** *Un ar bymtheg*

17 **Taen-a-Mimph** *Dau ar bymtheg*

18 **Tedder-a-Mimph** *Tri ar bymtheg*

19 **Medder-a-Mimph** *Pedwar ar bymtheg*

20 **Gigget** *Ugain*

Saxons advance

The English language has its basic grammar, its phonemes and stress, and about half its vocabulary from Anglo-Saxon. Old English was essentially the same as Old German, spoken by people from Angeln near the modern German-Danish border, and old Saxony. Nouns had three genders and four cases, and adjectives had to agree with nouns. For example the word for "sun" was feminine and had four different endings: it could be the subject of a verb (Nominative), the direct object of a verb (Accusative), the owner of another noun (Genitive), or the indirect object of a verb (Dative). Henry Sweet wrote the grammar of West Saxon at Oxford in 1882, and it looks just like a modern German grammar. The ending in the cases of the noun for "sun" are shown below.

Case Singular Plural

Nom sunn-e sunn-an

Acc sunn-an sunn-an

Gen sunn-an sunn-ena

Dat sunn-an sunn-um

Swedish, Afrikaans, Friesian, Yiddish and Modern English are also Germanic languages. The most influential OE dialect was West Saxon, especially after Alfred unified England in the war against the Danes. About four million words of Old English survive, and 90% of these are in West Saxon. The dialect of the North-East was Northumbrian, meaning north of the Humber and was never fully incorporated by Alfred. The vowel sounds of Northumbrian continue to give Lakeland language its distinctive quality.

The British people after Roman support ended around 450 CE were troubled by raiding parties of Picts and Scots. Hengist and Horsa - both words for stallions - were supposed to be the first Saxon mercenaries serving the British king Vortigern; however, all these people are rather mythological. Vortigern or some other Briton rashly asked foederati - people that acted as mercenaries to Rome - to help them. The successful Angles then sent back word that Britons were easy to defeat, and a larger migration of Angles, Jutes and Saxons followed. The remedy proved more troublesome than the disease, and soon the Britons had to fight for their own existence against these newcomers. Ambrosius Aurelianus (Emrys Wledig in Welsh) was a leader of the British resistance, according to the monk Gildas the Wise in his sermon *De Excidio et Conquestu Britanniae*. Ambrosius was Romano-British of high status, as Gildas describes him thus: "... a gentleman who, perhaps alone of the Romans, had survived the shock of this notable storm... his parents had worn the purple."

The Anglian kingdoms of Bernicia and Deira merged to become the kingdom of Northumbria, conquered the Britons of Elmet (the West Riding) in the early 600s, and expanded to include most of the North-East part of the British Isles. While the Celts struck back, winning a decisive battle at Mount Badon around 500 CE, the Anglo-Saxons continued to expand. The general trend was for the Welsh-speakers to be pushed westwards, into Cumbria, Wales, and Cornwall. The Anglo-Saxon kingdom of Northumbria would continue to press the Celts, including the Welsh-speaking peoples of Rheged and Strathclyde, the Gaelic-speaking people of Galloway and the Pictish speakers of the far North-East. The Saxons in their turn would later have to give ground to the Viking invasion.

English ceased to be the high language of England after 1066, although most people continued to speak one of its many dialects. Middle English rather suddenly lost two cases, gender and adjectival agreement around

1132 CE. One dialect based on Mercian re-emerged in 1425 for the purpose of writing laws so it is known as Chancery Standard English. There was very little inflectional morphology left, so that word order became essential for meaning.

Why did Middle English change so radically from Old English? The other language that has abandoned endings in favour of a word-order grammar - and probably for similar reasons - is Chinese. Under Norman rule Rouen French was used for government and Latin for religion and law, but most conversations still used words of English, often in a kind of a market-place pidgin, because one or both speakers were not fluently speaking their maternal language.

We can imagine a conversation like this at Appleby horse fair.

Saxon: "Wir offren thee diese Hengiste für only drei Gulden ; sie sind to den Plogh ausgebildeten".

Dane: "Du plogh horses they teeth are na good; we give two Gulder".

The Saxon will probably ignore the buyer's terrible English. In the process he picks up the Danish "they are" and eventually stops using his own "sie sind". He abandons attempts to use the compound verb ausbilden in its past participle meaning "trained to the plough" and says "we got him good for the plogh". Many compound OE verbs thus split into phrasal verbs that cannot be reunited. Now we can "take off clothes", but cannot "offtake clothes". Cumbrian manages to combine one phrasal verb back into a compound: "doff" the clothes is a contraction of "do-off"

You can now go quite along way in English with phrasal verbs based on "get" and a suitable preposition. Listen to this Modern English sentence:

"I get up at seven, get washed and dressed, get some cereal, then get off quick to get to work before it gets too busy ..." While this is perfectly good in the family or the pub, it would not be acceptable for a GCSE English essay. Then you would have to rewrite it using compound verbs derived from French, e.g. "After waking early I shower and dress, have breakfast and make a prompt departure to avoid traffic congestion ..."

This contrast between the "low" speech of home and farm and the "high" speech required for education, law and government gives Lakeland dialect its distinctive rural quality. Standard English uses vocabulary from French and classical languages, while the dialect uses words from two Germanic languages and avoids French, Latin and Greek. Cumbrian avoids French and uses short phrasal verbs, like this:

Ah gat up aboot sebben e' mworn, hed a wesh and donned me duds, gat mi poddish than set off gey sharp afoor t'rwoads gat ower thrang.

To read Jean's speech above, you have to learn the vowels. Current English accents nearly always keep the same consonants, but use a different set of vowels. For example, Mercian and Northumbrian had *ic (e)am* for "I am", while West Saxon had *ic eom* in the first person.

The small amount of preserved Northumbrian Old English is nearly all biblical. Bede's death song below is actually English, believe it or not! It includes the original letter ð for voiced "th".

> *Fore ðæm nedfere nænig wiorðe* Facing that enforced journey, no man can be
>
> *ðonc snottora ðon him ðearf sie* More prudent than he has good call to be
>
> *to ymbhycgenne ær his hinionge* If he consider, before his going hence
>
> *hwæt his gastæ godes oððe yfles* What for his spirit of good hap or of evil

æfter deað dæge doemed wiorðe After his day of death shall be determined.

The Scots dialect (or language) derived its phonemes mainly from Northumbrian Anglo Saxon. After a long separation of the Northumbrian Saxons forced by the Norse invasion, the languages merged again with the publication of the Knox bible in the 1600s, so that Scots became a dialect of English. Scots English remains closer to German than English does, preserving the "ch" sound and the rolled "r". Burns' poetry uses a Scots that was already archaic when he wrote it. "*Auld lang syne*" and "*Fair fa tha sonsie face*" sound quite German. There is only one word arguably from Gaelic - "sonsie", and could also be Norse for "plump".

The Saxons who came to dominate Westmorland were thus speakers of Old English with a Northumbrian accent. The Anglian settlers came into the area at the end of the seventh century. They infiltrated the eastern side of the Eden Valley via Stainmore and left place names that end in: *-ham, -ingham, -ington, and -ton*. The fact that they were stopped in their tracks so to speak can be seen by the string of such place names along foothills of the Pennines. The earliest recorded is **Addingham**. The names which end in -ingham and -ington follow personal names and means 'the town or hamlet of the people of X', so we read it backwards. Addingham is therefore 'the hamlet of the people of Addi'. There are also **Askham** (ash tree) and **Aldingham**.

Saxon place names often used the element *ton* (enclosure). There are 51 'tons' in the villages and towns of Westmorland. They include **Hilton** (hill), **Murton** (moor), **Dufton** (dove), **Orton** (ore), **Brampton** (brambles), **Long Marton** (mere), **Bolton** (a dwelling to which a farm has been added), all close together, with outliers such as **Plumpton** (plum), **Stainton** (stone); **Wigton** incorporates the Roman wick (*vicus*) or *wic* (farm). More examples are found on the west coast such as

Workington and in Low Furness; **Pennington**, and **Broughton**. Saxon elements in other parts of England often use *halh* (valley) or *lea* (meadow).

Writing was quite rare in early Anglo-Saxon times. Occasionally builders would cut their name on a beam, or a gravestone would be marked using the Norse runic script. The set of runic characters was called a futhorc, named from the first six characters, rather as the word "alphabet" is named from the first two Greek characters. The runic inscription in Carlisle cathedral seems to refer to a Viking massacre.

The main incentive to writing was the adoption of Christianity. The new religion was brought to the region by Irish monks. In 685, King Ecgfrith of Northumbria granted Carlisle plus fifteen miles around to St Cuthbert together with Cartmel together with all its British inhabitants; the Saint visited Carlisle in the same year. There was a short period when Anglo Saxon was written with the Irish uncial script, before it was replaced by Roman letters.

The Ruthwell Cross is rather curious piece of writing in small church just over the border in Scotland. The image below copies the runes which are written plough-wise around a stone pillar. On the right is a transliteration into the Roman alphabet, including the ash and thorn letters. It is the story of Jesus on the cross, but written in runic, anachronistically for the 8th century. It appears to be set up outside a church to address pagans, in the slight hope that they could read it! The same evangelical purpose is found elsewhere in the dream of the rood. It is a hero-warrior parody of the crucifixion story, but told by a talking tree cross!

Northumbrians, Britons and Norse co-existed in North-West England, recognising others' boundaries. **Walney Island** and **Walna Scar** on Coniston fells both say "of the Saxons' (genitive case)". **Cumberland** was recognised by Northumbrians as mainly British. These three peoples eventually came to speak the same version of Middle English. The imposition of French as the high language by the Normans - yet another group of migrants from Scandinavia - had little effect on the vernacular language.

The adoption of English as the high language of England after 1425 had a much more dramatic effect. In common with every other dialect and accent of English, Lakeland speech is now dragged along with innovations in English, which is now the second language for much of the world and first language for several huge populations. Innovations have included these: abbreviations such as "can't" and "doesn't" from American; the loss of "ch" and "r"; na-whit" became "not" in Standard English, though the older -na after the verb may still be heard. Dialect speakers learn to "code switch" - using London English with outsiders, but Lakes English on the farm, in the playground and at home.

ᚪᚱᛁᛋᛏ ᚹᚫᛋ ᚪᚾ
Krist wæs on

ᚱᚪᛞᛁ
rodi

ᚻᚹᛖᚦᚱᚫ ᚦᛖᚱ ᚹᚢᛋᚫ
Hweþræ þer fusæ

ᚹᛏᚱᚱᚪᚾ ᚪᛈᚫᚢᚾ
fearran kwomu /
ᚪᛈᚫᚢᚾ /

ᚪᛞᚦᛁᛚᚪ   ᛏᛁᛚ
æþþilæ   *til*
ᚪᚾᚢᛗ
anum

Iceland is born

The people of Scandinavia (with the exception of Finland) all spoke the same language, with some local variations. As Denmark was the centre, the language was often simply called 'Danish' (*donsk tunga*). We could call it Old Danish, but could also Old Norse, or Scandinavian, or North Germanic. "Viking" is not basically an ethnic group, but a decision to live by raiding.

Icelandic stayed fairly close to the Danish tongue, while Modern Danish and other parts of Scandinavia differentiated away from it. Differentiation into East Norse, West Norse and Gutnish came after the period of colonisation of Iceland and Britain. Old East Norse was spoken in what we now call Denmark, Sweden and North-East England. Old West Norse was spoken in Norway, Iceland, and colonies on the west side of the British Isles, including Cumbria. There was a further dialect called Gutnish or Gothic on the island of Gotland, another in the Crimea, and Norse would have been understood to some extent in the low countries.

Ships were essential for movement around Norway, where transport over land was very difficult. Longships were generally clinker built with broad beam. The most ambitious was the *knarr*, built for Atlantic voyages. They were cargo ships averaging a length of about 54 feet (16 metres), and a hull capable of carrying up to 122 tons. *Knerrir* routinely crossed the North Atlantic centuries ago carrying livestock and stores to Greenland. They were capable of sailing 75 miles in one day and held a crew of about 20-30. Rowing was the means of propulsion in inshore waters, but a single sail was used for longer journeys. Amazingly, the sails were made of wool! The *Spælsau* sheep gives *Wadmal* (Old Norse *vaðmál* wool. The Icelandic sheep (Icelandic: *íslenska sauðkindin*) is derived from the sheep brought by the first settlers. Icelandic fleece is dual-coated. In Icelandic the long outer coat is called *tog* and the fine inner coat *þel*.

The Viking expansion was by water. Raids and subsequent colonisation of the British Isles was via the North Sea and Atlantic. The Atlantic was also the route to Iceland, Greenland and even America. The shallow draft of the longships and the fact that they could be carried allowed movement right across continental Europe. The Volga and Dnieper rivers were arteries to the Black and Caspian seas, so there are colonies along them, in brown on the map. The cataracts of the Dnieper were given Norse names such as *Oulvorsi* (Old Norse *holmfors*, "island rapid") and *Stroukoun* (Old Norse *strukum*, "rapid current"). There were places where the ship was ported. A similar portage has been identified at Drigg in west Cumbria. Many familiar words attest the linguistic heritage of Norse movement. The Old Norse feminine noun *víking* refers to "an expedition overseas". Vikings who served as mercenaries in Constantinople were known in Greek as "Varangian", from *vár*, "pledge, faith" and "*gengi*" 'companion', thus meaning 'sworn companion, confederate'. The root Rus in Russia, Belarus and other place names is likely to derive from an old Norse term for "the men who row" (*rods-*). This would then be the same as the Finnish and Estonian names for Sweden: *Ruotsi* and *Rootsi*. Many peoples of Eastern Europe have "*slav*" in their name. This could derive either from the words "word" or "slave". Vikings clearly captured people to sell as slaves on their journeys to the Black Sea.

The Volga trade route was established by the Varangians who settled in North western Russia in the early 9th century. They established a settlement called Ladoga (Old Norse: *Aldeigjuborg*), about six miles south of the Volkhov River's entry into Lake Ladoga. The Volga trade route lost its importance by the 11th century owing to the decline of silver output from Baghdad. The Icelandic saga *Yngvars saga víðförla* (Ingvar the far-travelled) describes an expedition of Swedes around 1041 via the Volga then the Caspian into the land of the Saracens (*Serkland*).

The expedition was unsuccessful, and afterwards no attempts were made to reopen the route between the Baltic and Caspian seas by the Norsemen. The route down the Dnieper to the Black Sea and the Byzantine Empire gained more weight.

At the western extremity of Norse influence, *Vinland* is the area south of the St. Lawrence river. It includes Nova Scotia and *Markland* - the area now known as Labrador. This Norse presence in North America is recorded in the Greenlanders' saga and Erik the Red's saga - two versions of the same story. The first describes a voyage made by Bjarni Herjolfsson and the subsequent voyages of Leif Eriksson. The sagas are full of lineage, and it is interesting to read that these two key figures had connections to Ireland and the Western Isles of Scotland. We read that Thorfinn Karlsefni was descended from Aud the Deep Minded, a Viking queen in Dublin and settler in west Iceland, and Karval, King of Ireland. Gudrid Thorbjarnardottir was descended from a Gaelic slave brought to Iceland by the same Aud and was born and raised in Iceland. The Newfoundland village of L'Anse aux Meadows is the location of *Leifsbudir* (Leif's Camp). *Kjarlaness* (Keel Point), the Norse settlement in Vinland, is now called Cape Breton. *Straumsfjord* and *Straumsey* (*straum* meaning 'stream' in this instance) are on the north of the Bay of Fundy. Further south is the settlement called *Hóp* meaning 'tidal pool', now New York.

The settlement of Iceland is conventionally dated to 874 CE and the first settler is named as Ingólfur Arnarson. The island was known much earlier, as the classical writer Pytheas may have been describing it when he spoke of a land called Thule. A further tradition is that Icelanders are of pure Norse descent. This view is expounded in the *lándnamabók*. Reality is more complicated. There had probably been Irish monks there before Arnarson, and the first settlers may have been as much British as Norse. By 930 the Icelandic population is estimated as 25,000 settlers.

The Norse settlement of Iceland after 874 is nearly contemporaneous with the Norse settlement of North-West England.

The expansion of the Norse population in the ninth century is something of a puzzle. Norway proper has very little arable land, so food shortage becomes an issue. On the other hand agriculture was successful in Denmark and Sweden and no famine has been demonstrated. Retaliation against Charlemagne for forced Christianisation is another possibility, but if vengeance were the motive, why attack England rather than the Franks? Emigration of the "youth bulge" would be usual, but again there is little evidence for a sudden population increase. Another motive for the exodus from Norway was to escape from Harold Fairhair and taxation. Shortage of wives has been advanced as a hypothesis by James Bennett. This wife-shortage hypothesis also implies infanticide of female children.

The continental divide was chosen as the location for the Icelandic ting

Genetics has shown that the male settlers of Iceland were overwhelmingly Scandinavian, but the female settlers were overwhelmingly British. The word "British" here means genetically Celtic and speaking p-Celtic (Welsh) or q-Celtic (Irish and Scots Gaelic), or lost variations such as Cumbric or Pictish. This discovery depends on two sex-linked sets of genes: while most DNA is inherited with equal probability from both parents, the Y-chromosome is inherited via the paternal line, and mitochondrial DNA only via the maternal line. Research by Goodacre, Helgason in 2005 showed heritability this way: Scandinavian DNA on the Y-chromosome was 0.75 and mitochondrial DNA 0.34; British DNA on the Y-chromosome was 0.25, but mitochondrial DNA 0.66. This last 0.66 statistic is amazing. Put simply, the men who settled Iceland were ethnically Norse, although they may have started from any point on the Iceland bus route in Britain or Scandinavia. Their wives were likely to have come from North-West Britain or Ireland.

How numerous were the Scandinavians in Cumbria? In the research of David Goldstein of University College London, the Y-chromosomes of men in various part of the British Isles was compared with that of Viking areas. This was reported by the BBC television series 'Blood of the Vikings'. As Norse and Saxon Y-chromosomes were rather similar, the statistical analysis was between two groups only: "Britons" and "invaders". The Scottish mainland and southern England had a mixture, while York and the Northern Isles were high on Viking DNA. Penrith had the highest result of DNA links to Norwegian Vikings in the whole of Britain. In Ireland only a few miles out of Dublin virtually no Viking DNA was detected.

Did the women emigrants from Britain leave any trace? The Icelandic children of these unions might have heard their mothers' Welsh or Irish as small infants, but West Norse when their fathers came home. The two parental languages are analogous to the mixed language pattern known as Michif, spoken by children of Cree women who married French trappers. In Michif the nouns are mostly French, but the verbs tend to use Cree grammar. We are not aware of systematic research on Icelandic grammar that might show Celtic patterns, but here are some possibilities. Icelandic tends to use continuous forms of the present tense, as Welsh does. For example, *ætlum við að fara í ferðalag* ("we are going on a journey"), whereas Norwegian might use a simple present. There might also be phonetic traces. One intriguing sound is the Icelandic "ll". The final sound in *"jökull"* (glacier) seems to be the same lateral fricative found in Welsh (e.g. *pwll, allt*), but not in other Scandinavian or indeed European languages.

How did British women arrive in Iceland as partners of Norse men? Given the Vikings' reputation for force, we might imagine it was not a matter of choice. Yet there was some affinity between Britons and Scandinavians against Anglo-Saxons. The 10th century Welsh poem *Armes Prydein* (English: The 'Prophesy of Britain') imagines Cadwallon and Cadwaladr as Welsh leaders of a union of all Celts and Norsemen driving the *Saesneg* back into the sea. Rheged was annexed by Saxons around 730 CE, although Strathclyde held on till about 1050. British women may have decided Norsemen were a lesser evil than Saxons as husbands. We know from the Greenlanders saga of two Celtic women: Aud, an aristocrat and Gudrid, a slave. There is therefore a strong connection between Cumbria and Iceland, in both directions.

The linguistic part of this connection is the persistence of 9th century West Norse in both areas. There may be a couple of hundred West Norse words found in farming, place names and general vocabulary in both Iceland and Cumbria. Icelanders have made strenuous efforts to keep their language unchanged, so Lakeland speech is now actually closer to that of Iceland than that of Denmark or Norway. Iceland was quite isolated for several centuries while under Danish rule. Poverty and famine occurred during these centuries, partly because Denmark tried to keep a monopoly of sea trade, but then neglected to send ships. The only source of timber for years at a time was driftwood. There were always contacts by sea, sometimes clandestine. One improbable contact language was a Basque-Icelandic pidgin used between whalers in the 17th century.

After a period of borrowing, a linguistic purism movement developed in the 18th century. To incorporate new technology into Iceland, archaic words are recycled. Whereas most languages have adopted the word "computer", Icelandic rediscovered two words: "*tala*" ('number') and "*völva*" ('prophetess') to make "*tölva*". "*Simi*" is an ancient word meaning 'thread' and is now used for 'telephone'. This was introduced just in time for mobile phones with no cord! A helicopter is a "*þyrla*" ('whirler') and a jet aircraft is a "*þota*" ('zoomer'). Linguistic conservatism became a matter of national pride in Iceland, particularly after sovereignty in 1918 and independence from Denmark in 1944. In Cumbria the conservatism was because West Norse is used where the dominating effect of English is least - in farming, place names and between mother and child.

The stress patterns may also be similar. Stress is quite hard to pin down, but the stress of Germanic languages becomes very clear in alliterative verse. We now think of poetry in Romance-language terms, with final rhyming sounds. French tends to stress syllables equally, but Germanic languages have initial stressed syllables followed by a variable number of unstressed syllables. Alliterative verse used this feature to make oral history easier to remember. Each pair of lines has a head letter, which is repeated in the pair. Each line is divided into two half lines, with a definite break in the middle. There must be two stressed and two unstressed syllables. Alliteration is similar in Old Saxon, Old Icelandic, and Old High German. Old English (i.e. Old Saxon) used this convention, and there is one main saga that has survived - Beowulf. Here is a section describing the ogre, from Chapter XI, line 710:

Ða com of more under misthleoþum

Grendel gongan, .godes yrre bær;

mynte se manscaða manna cynnes

sumne besyrwan in sele þam hean.

A speaker of modern German now finds this easier than a speaker of modern English. In modern English this would be: "Then from the moorland, by misty crags, with God's wrath laden, Grendel came. The monster was minded of mankind now sundry to seize in the stately house."

Icelandic pronunciation is challenging, but the text is relatively easy once a few accents are learned. The Latin alphabet was adopted for writing the bible at the *althingi* ('parliament') of 1000 CE, when the country became officially Christian, almost overnight. It retains the characters ð and þ, the voiced and unvoiced "th" sounds, that occur in Beowulf but have been dropped from English. Accents are used over some vowels: ú, ó and á are longer than their counterparts without the accent. The ö is similar to the German vowel in Österreich (Austria). The interested reader can study Online Icelandic - a well-structured, free, and helpful language course.

The Icelandic sagas were written down around the 12th century, but incorporated much older oral history. The continuity of the language means that the sagas can still be read, albeit with some footnotes, by most Icelanders. The use of common language instead of Latin makes Icelandic unusual in this time. Are the influences of Celtic oral history-telling still detectable? There are research questions for linguists. The following verse is from Egil's saga by Egil Skallagrimsson. The "st" sound occurs three times in the first two lines. Additional rhyming is achieved also by internal rhyme such as the repeated "fn" sound.

Þél höggr stórt fyr stáli

stafnkvígs á veg jafnan

út með éla meitli

andærr jötunn vandar,

en svalbúinn selju

sverfr eirar vanr þeiri

Gestils ölpt með gustum

gandr of stál fyr brandi.

This passage is describing headwind and snow buffeting the planks of a longship. A literal translation of it would be incomprehensible, because the word order is hugely altered and a metaphor called kenning is used. For example the fourth line *andærr jötunn vandar* is literally "rowing against, giant/enemy, mast" which is a metaphor for "headwind".

The common influence of West Norse in Cumbria and Iceland helps the Cumbrian traveller. Jack Manning asserts that he could make himself understood by speaking his Flookburgh dialect to Icelanders. After trekking the *Laugavegur* ('hot spring trail') trail in Iceland, one of the authors assembled these photos that you might be able to read. Sometimes Icelandic is easier, and in other places Nynorsk is closer to Cumbrian English.

We have developed some parallels in the settlement by Vikings of Iceland and Cumbria. The continuing connections will be explored further in the next chapter.

Scandinavian signs a Cumbrian might read

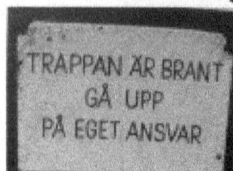

TRAPPAN ÄR BRANT
GÅ UPP
PÅ EGET ANSVAR

REYKJAVÍK

Álftavatn

Leikskólinn
Háaleiti

BJÖRGUNARVESTI
ERU UNDIR SÆTUNUM!

Jökulinn er varasamur yfirferðar.
Víða leynast hættulegar sprungur
sem sjást oft ekki fyrr en
um seinan. Leitið leiðsagnar.

Bredenbecksmauet

Snæfellsjökull

Vaðið krefst varúðar

- MOBICO NORWAY -
FLYTTING MELLOM NORGE OG SPANIA

- Flytting inn og utland
- Pakking av flyttegods
- Lagring
- Flyttevask
- Kontorflyttinger
- Lagring
- Transporttjenester

MOBICO - NORGE - OSLO

Norsemen reach Cumbria

The settlement of Iceland was close in time to the Scandinavian settlement of the Lake District. The Scandinavian settlement of the Lake District is most notable in the place names. There are many physical survivals too, such as the hog back gravestones, wheel-headed crosses and carved stones. Finally, and the most fascinating is the heritage of the vernacular speech; for the dialects of the old counties of Cumberland, Westmorland and the Furness peninsula are rich in words that originate from Norway, Iceland and Denmark.

We know that the first recorded Scandinavian invasion into the region was in 867AD when Halfden the Dane overthrew and destroyed Carlisle (Caer-Luel or Luel's fort). He and his army returned in 875 and attacked the city again. The Danish infiltrated over the Pennines from Yorkshire and developed settlements, one of the test words being place names ending in þorp (thorp). Only three are to be found in the old county of Westmorland: Crackenthorpe and Hackthorpe in the Eden Valley and Milnthorpe in the south of the county.

The Vikings had a reputation for vicious raids; and many have been recorded along the east coast and all around Scotland and the Western Isles. They arrived near Dublin about 837 when 60 ships were recorded in the River Liffey and 60 more in the River Boyne. They built fortified settlements near Dublin in 841. This Irish occupancy did not last very long as they were expelled by the Irish in 902 and it is believed that some settled in Cumbria at that time.

The Heimkringla Saga of the Icelandic historian Snorri Sturluson tells that problems arose between Harald Fairhair, King of Norway and the Scandinavian colonists in Orkney, Shetland, the Hebrides and Isle of Man. It appears that these people had got a bit 'above themselves' and sent raiding parties to the Norwegian coasts! This action goaded Harald into launching an expedition against the rebels, and in AD 895 a fleet of Viking ships from Norway harried the western seaboard of Scotland, but news of Harald's action reached the Isle of Man before his warships and, according to Snorri: "then fled all folk into Scotland, and the island was unpeopled of men: all goods that might be shifted and flitted away. So when Harald's folk went a-land they took no booty". The saga specifies Scotland as the refuge, but remember that Cumberland was part of Scotland until William Rufus advanced on Carlisle in 1092. Although Snorri wrote the saga in the early 13th century, he was probably using the old political geography.

Norsemen had become established in the Isle of Man. A boat burial at Balladoole has been dated to the late 9th or early 10th century. Their influence in the Manx lifestyle still survives today in their judiciary system of Tynwald. From the Isle of Man these people would have looked across the Irish Sea to the coast of Cumberland just 22 miles away. It is quite possible that some small groups would have travelled there to explore the land, and create small settlements, an easy move for people with long-honed seagoing skills. The main influx came between 925 and 930 when they fled from the Isle of Man in a mass exodus. The Ynglinga Saga printed by the Manx Society in 1860 tells us that in the late ninth century the Scandinavian peoples in the Isle of Man set up an autonomous government.

Gudrodr Olafson died in 1187 and the Manx people asked his son Rognvaldr to be their king. He visited King John in 1205 and obtained grants of lands in Lancashire. His brother was Olafr and internecine war existed between the two between 1187 and 1229 over the kingship of Man. In 1212 Olafr killed Rognvaldr's son when he captured him on St Columba's Isle, Skye and mutilated him. In retribution Rognvaldr burned all Olafr's ships in a night time raid on St. Patricks Isle, Peel. Fishing rights around the Isle of Man were granted to Holm Cultram Abbey in 1229. In the same year Olafr granted licence to purchase 60 head of cattle or equivalent to St Bees priory. King Rognvaldr of Man was killed by his brother Olafr in 1229 and is buried at Furness Abbey. Olafr died in 1237 and is buried at Rushen Castle, Castletown, and the last King of Man, Magnus Olafsson died at Rushden in 1265.

Norsemen from the Ise of Man fled in their *knerrir* to Cumbria

The area was still not peaceful, as Eric Bloodaxe, the last Viking King of York was killed on Stainmore in 954. He was the son of Harold Fairhair. Eric was also King of Norway c930 to 936. In about 1000 King Olaf Tryggvason plundered Cumberland among other places, and Ethelred marched to Cumberland "and laid waste very nearly the whole of it ". The Scandinavian culture remained important, for in 1163, a committee of thirty sworn men witnessed a document that divided the Furness fells between the Abbot of Furness and the Baron of Kendal; over half of the witnesses were of Scandinavian origin, with names such as Swein, Ravenkill, Ketel, Ulf, Orm and Gospatrick - the latter being a Norse-Irish name. According to legend, the last Scandinavian stronghold was in Buttermere, where the settlers held out against the Norman invasion.

It is therefore plausible that the refugees from Harald Fairhair's wrath would flee to Cumbria. Certainly, they must have known the coastal area around Morecambe Bay and inlets along the Cumbria coast, and it is likely that some of their kinsmen had already settled there. Another point is this: if these Norse-Irish people had come to Cumbria as hostile invaders, surely they would have destroyed the existing Anglian villages and erased their place-names. This did not occur; for on the Cumbrian coastal plain Scandinavian and earlier Anglian names co-exist in close proximity, and this could indicate racial harmony and a peaceful influx of Norse-Irish refugees. From the Cumbrian coast there are many rivers leading up fjord-like valleys to mountains; to any of these new settlers this topography is reminiscent of the Norwegian homeland of their forelders ('parents'). This was good farming land, with plenty of grazing, and timber.

Some of the Viking legacy in the form of stone carvings and crosses include those at Gosforth in West Cumbria where a slender and magnificent cross of red sandstone 4.4 metres high has stood in the churchyard for over 1,000 years; it was carved by people of Norse-Irish descent and shows on its east side scenes from the life of Christ, whilst the other three sides have representations from pagan Norse mythology including the gods Loki, Hiemdal and Vidar, as well as dragons and serpents; it is interpreted as representing Ragnarok, the overthrow of the old gods and the triumph of the White Christ and incorporates the Norse ash tree Yggdrasil. Also at Gosforth in the church are three more Viking carvings. The Fishing Stone is believed to be part of another cross; this shows a hart trampling a serpent or snake, and below is an illustration from a story well-known throughout Scandinavia of the god Thor fishing for the World Serpent. The warrior's tomb stone is a hogback grave stone, showing on one side two armies, equipped with round shields and weapons, facing each other, and may commemorate a great battle. The third stone is also a hog back referred to as the Saint's

Tomb, the name probably deriving from the carving of the crucifixion on one end.

At Kirkby Stephen in the church, there is another carved stone known as the Bound Devil, it shows a horned and bearded figure bound hand and foot, this is likely to Norse god Loki, who for his involvement in the death of Balder was bound and thrown into a snake pit. At Penrith a group consisting of four weathered hogback stones and the shafts of two wheel headed crosses, form what is known as the Giant's Grave and is reputedly the resting place of Owen Caesarious, a famous warrior connected to the Kingdom of Rheged.

Hogback gravestones represent the houses of the dead, resembling upturned boats with shingle roofs, and examples are to be found in several old churches around the county. Norse crosses and carved stones can also be found in churches such as Dearham near Maryport and Aspatria.

The survival of Scandinavian-type runes in to the 12th century proves that a form of Norse was still being written as well as spoken. One of the finest examples is to be found on the font in Bridekirk church; in Furness, a runic inscription on a tympanum at Pennington church dates from around 1160, and at Urswick church, in 1911 an ancient carved stone was found incorporated in the wall. It is known as the Tunwinni Cross, and is carved with a panel containing runes, below which are two figures. The stone was dated by the antiquarian W. G. Collingwood to the 9th century. In 1909 another stone had been found, this one being a fragment of the cross-shaft dating possibly from the 10th century. Finally, the Dolfin Stone in Carlisle cathedral, translates as 'Dolfin wrait this a this stane', like an early example of graffiti.

Other physical artefacts include finds from the Cumwhitton area that included funerary goods; and Hutton in the Forest where two warrior graves were discovered in 1822. A silver Irish-Norse penanular brooch was discovered on Orton Scar, and a Viking sword at Witherslack. With the advent of metal detecting, it is likely that more will come to light.

The Scandinavian judiciary system is also represented in two possible thing mounds. These are similar to Tynwald Hill in the Isle of Man, and were the site of law-making gatherings. One is at Fell Foot, Little Langdale, and was identified by W. G. Collingwood. The other is west of Shap, it was originally known as *Thengheved* (later **Theafstead**) and is mentioned in the grant of lands for Shap Abbey in 1199; it lies near the small settlement of **Tailbert**, a name coming from *tjald-borg* or tent-burgh, the place where tents were pitched for the Thing. This is not unlike **Tilberthwaite** in Langdale, close to the other site. This system of gathering at a set place for judicial reasons continued for centuries with manor courts, some of which still operate.

The form of old Danish that influenced Lakeland may have come from the west coast of Norway, which has retained dialect differences from standard Norwegian (Bokmål). Test words for West Norse are **thwaite** (*þveit*), **booth** (*buthir*), **gill**, **beck** (stream), **force** (*foss*), **fell** (*fjäll*), **tarn** (*tjörn*) and **dale** (*dalr*) - all widespread. There are differences from fjord to fjord, but some Norwegian counties on the west-central coast have voted that they should be officially referred to as Nynorsk (new Norwegian), the name given by Ivar Aasen. Nynorsk retains masculine, feminine and neuter, whereas Bokmål and Danish now have only two genders. 12% of Norwegians and three counties have declared for Nynorsk: Hordaland, Møre og Romsdal and Sogn og Fjordane. The use of the word 'beck' for a stream is thought to be only between the Hardanger and Sogne fjords – the most likely origin of the forefathers of our first Scandinavian settlers.

Place names in Cumbria will indicate what was once in a *thwaite*, which means a clearing or enclosure. In many place names which end in thwaite it will indicate a) what was cleared, b) what it was cleared for, c) the owner of the clearing or d) a description of its location. Examples of the first set: **Thornthwaite, Bowderthwaite, Stonethwaite, Rounthwaite** (rowans), and **Brackenthwaite.** Examples of the second set: **Haverthwaite** (oats), **Crosthwaite** (cross), **Applethwaite** (apples) **Cornthwaite, Calthwaite** (calf), **Rossthwaite** (horse). In the third set are: **Finsthwaite, Ullthwaite.** In the final set are: **Southwaite, Braithwaite, Micklethwaite, Mirethwaite.** Local people rarely pronounce the element 'thwaite', but instead say 'thet'.

Stockmen in those times moved uphill in spring for fresh grazing, a practice known as transhumance. In Welsh the term is *hafod.* The outlying Norse booths (*buthir*) and huts (*scalar*) survive in place names which include -booth or -scale. Saeters and shielings are indicated in two ways by the ending *erg, ergh* or *er* or by *satter* sett seat or side. Examples can be demonstrated with **Mosser, Birker, Docker, Skelsmergh, and Sizergh.** Then there are **Ambleside, Rayside, Selside, Seat Sandal, Hawkshead, Seatoller and Setterah.** Saeters or sheilings still survive from this period in among other places, **Whelter Combe** above the Haweswater reservoir. Whelter - *hvilfter* means a hollow or combe with shieling.

The Ting mound in Little Langdale

The names of animals, both wild and domestic, are commonplace: *svina* (swine) to be found in **Swindale**, *griss* (piglet) to be found in **Grisedale**, *gas* (geese) to be found in **Gaisgill**, *hjartar* (hart or deer) to be found in **Harter Fell**, *hross* (horse) as in **Rosthwaite** and **Rosgill**. Swans were seen on **Elterwater** - *elptavatn* the lake of the swans, a place that still attracts migrating Whooper swans from Scandinavia and Iceland. There is another swan lake *Aftavatn* on the Laugavegur trail in Iceland.

By indicates a farmstead, though probably in Danish rather than West Norse. In **Appleby** (apple farm), **Kirkby Stephen** (Stephens church farm) **Kirkby Thore** (Thor's church farm), **Crosby Ravensworth** (Ravens farm with crosses). **Langwathby** (farm by the long *wath* or ford) **Lazonby** incorporates the word *leysinger* meaning freedman so means 'freedman's farm'; compare that with **Bomby** (near Bampton) meaning bondman's farm. The name *keld* used alone or as an ending means a spring and is Icelandic; there is a Keld near Shap where the hamlet has grown around a copious perpetual spring that still yields the loveliest of water. **Threlkeld** is the spring of the *thralls* (slaves). There are also a large number of placenames ending in –by in the Carlisle area, all attached to Germanic personal names: **Botcherby, Etterby, Harraby, Upperby, Rickerby and Tarraby.** Examples in the Penrith area include **Johnby, Ellonby, Lamonby, Motherby** and **Hornby.**

The grant of lands for Shap Abbey positively bristles with Scandinavian place names; **Karlwath** (the ford of the carls or husbandmen), **Keld, Langshabeck, Rasat** incorporates the *set* or *saeter,* **Lowther** (*laudr-á* or foamy river), **Rosgill** - the gill where horses were to be found, **Creskeld** the spring where cress grows, **Alinbalike** (*balkr* Icel. for balk or fence), **Thamboord** (the dale of the gut or bowstring - compare with *Thambardal* in Iceland), **Binbarh** (*bingr* Icel. - *bing,* bolster and *barh,* like the ergh shieling), *Thengeheved* (see previous paragraph), **Swindale** (pig valley).

Norsemen never dominated in Cumbria, but they did in many other places. Vikings travelled further south, attacking Paris from 840 onwards. Rollo agreed a military service for land deal with the king of France, thus founding Normandy in northern France about 911. The Normans (Northmen) who invaded England in 1066 were descendants of the Norwegian Vikings, although they spoke Rouen French by this time. More Normans, including the de Brus lineage, moved to Scotland in 1155, again to seek land titles in exchanged for military service.

So the Iceland bus moved Norsemen all over Europe, as well as some Britons. In the final chapter we will try to see how Cumbrian speech reflects this ethnic history.

The Grammar of Lakeland Language

We saved the technical linguistics till the end, for those readers who have persevered this far!

The speech of the Lakes is a source of delight to people born to it, but has received rather less attention from linguists. We are fortunate to have William Dickinson's 1859 Glossary of the Dialect of Cumberland, Robert Ferguson's 1873 "Dialect of Cumberland", and William Rollinson's "The Cumbrian Dictionary of Dialect, Tradition and Folklore", among others. Jack Manning more recently found some additional words in South Cumbrian coastal dialect. The Lakeland Dialect Society's web-site gives a comprehensive listing of all these sources. Dialect dictionaries are essentially word lists. But what is a "word"? As we work though Jack Manning's list, some Flookburgh words clearly are not connected with standard English: **allekur** - sour, a vinegary beer; **attepile** - a stinging fish, the lesser weaver. Many are elisions made during rapid speech, e.g "mummel" for "mumble"; some are general English slang; and others are vowel variants of words in general English. These vowel variations are of most interest. Cumbria has been rather a long way from university linguistic departments and has not received the attention it deserves. In this chapter we make some attempt to define the accent of Lakeland language.

The linguist de Saussure distinguished diachronic and synchronic approaches to linguistics. The first involves history and etymology. Lakes speech gives clues to the history of its people. It has evolved through the interplay of Anglo-Saxon and Norse, with some contribution from Welsh. Historical questions include the Great Vowel Shift (GVS) which occurred in later Middle English. All the vowels of standard English changed between the time of Chaucer and that of Shakespeare. Chaucer lived in what would have sounded like a *hoos*, with his *weef*, and *hay* would romance *heer* with a bottle of *weena*, drunk by the light of the *moan*. Two hundred years later Shakespeare would have pronounced them in more or less the modern way, as "house, wife, he, her, wine, and moon". The GVS had less effect on Northumbrian-accented English.

Synchronic linguistic topics include phonetics, stress, morphology and syntax. Cumbrian speech has very distinctive phonetics, but is fairly close to standard English in its morphology and syntax. It differs from the phonetics of RP (Received Pronunciation, i.e. standard English) mainly in its vowels, as do most English regional accents. A vowel is produced by air coming up from the lungs making the vocal folds vibrate. The pitch of the vowel is fixed by the size of the space between the tongue and the roof of the mouth. This makes a resonant cavity, just like a guitar box does for the strings. Vowels can be described mostly by tongue position: CLOSE-OPEN and FRONT-BACK on the diagram below.

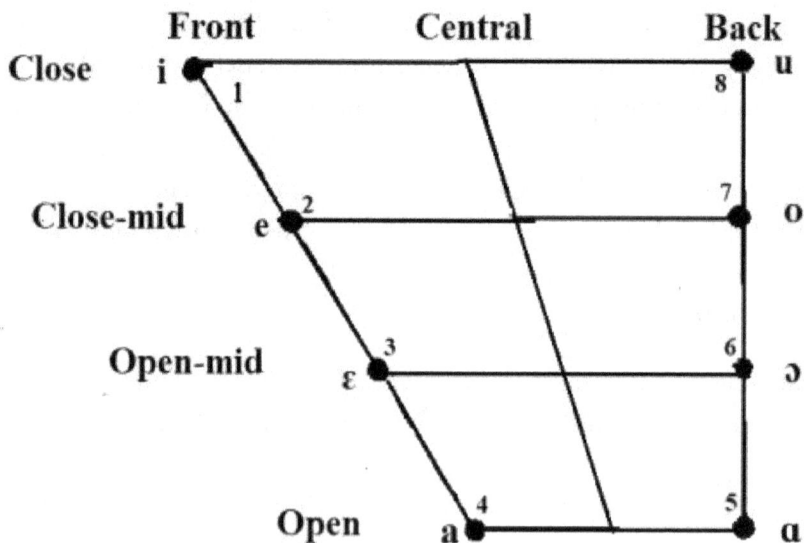

If the tongue is up near the top teeth, a high-pitched "ee" sound is made (the light tongue in the left-hand picture). In the diagram on the right below, the first cardinal vowel is represented by the IPA symbol "i" and is described as front close. The sequence of vowels by convention starts at front-close, then works anti-clockwise round the mouth. If the tongue is low and down at the back of the mouth, an "ɑ" is made; (this is different from "a"). This vowel is at the bottom right and is described as back-open. Continuing the anti-clockwise movement the final vowel is the back-close "oo".

Professor Wells and linguists at University College London tried to reduce the enormous complexity of speech sounds into a smaller number of "phonemes". When trying to list the above vowels, we were reminded of trying to sort out foreign stamps without always being able to read the country names. Only when we learnt that "Helvetia" was the Latin name for Switzerland could we use that page of the album.

According to the UCL theory, English usually has 20 vowel phonemes. This may come as surprising statement to the reader who remembers learning only five vowels at school! To understand, we have to examine the implicit rules by which we construct speech. Think of a phoneme as a speech unit that could be inserted between "b" and "d" to make a new word. By including some obscure words such as "Boyd" and "Buddhist" you might find 14 or 15; another four could be made between a "b" and an American final "r" or English "ee-ŭ", such as "beer" and "byre". Northern English is described as having 19 vowel phonemes, as it does not differentiate "foot" and "strut" as Southern English does. Each of these 19 vowels make a new word, and so are called phonemes. Professor Wells has given comprehensive accounts of English accents, though Leeds may be nearest comparison for Cumbria.

Lance Porter wrote one of the first pieces in dialect speech for the Lakeland Dialect Society back in 1939. He wrote his dialect speech using intuitive letter combinations, as Anglo-Saxon writers did. Listen to the vowels in his call for people to join the Lakeland Dialect Society.

We're nut stuck up er prood i't mooth,

Fer t'main on us wer bred in't fells.

We're nobbut wiet, yammly fwoak

Off t'seam switch as yersels.

An' like yersels, we clag tight tull

O't bits o' country ways an' looar;

We like ta hod a crack aboot

T'' auld dale-fwoak 'at hev gone afooar.

Ort roads the' meead, an' t' wo's the' built

An' t' neames the' cawt ther' yams an' teuls,

An' t' sangs an' teals o't Shippard meets,

An' t' geames t'barnes laiked at t'sceuls.

Mi fadder, (an' nea doot he's reet),

Sez t's main o' t' fell fwoak er o't seame

They "Hawk tagidder" on a drag

Till Foxy's brush is hung on t'beame.

He sez 'at t'interest (like t' auld Fox)

Is rousan' noo fer thee an' me,

Soo join, yersels, an git yer kin

Ta join oor own Society.

There a few words in this that do not occur in standard English: lake, barns, and possibly clag and crack; words of French origin are almost absent, except *société*; but most of the other divergences from RP are the vowels. In modern linguistic theory, every fluent speaker of a dialect has a set of rules, including phonetic rules. These rules are not explicit, so they have to be teased out. Our fluent speaker at present is Jean Scott-Smith, whose vowels are those of North Westmorland. They are a little different from those used above by Lance Porter, who grew up in Eskdale. The 19 vowel phonemes may be these:

eeă mead, seam, nea, speean

ee reet, theer, deef

eu sceul, feul, beut, beuk

ĕ fer, bred

ĭ (short) tagidder, shippard, built, git

ay ways, main, teym, seyd

ăĭ like, time

ă (short) lang, wrang, fadder, an

æ taele,

aa laal, ah've

ŏ (short) hod, o't (of)

ō (long) home, bone, stone

or coa, caw'd, (called) o't, aw (all)

oa cwoat (coat)

ŭ tull (until), hung

oy boil, oyster, join

yūĭ buik (book)

ooă afooar, looar (lore), nooat, booas

oo hoose, doot

eeă This vowel diphthong is also found in Geordie. RP used to have it, but lost it: "meat" and "meet' now sound the same, though the spelling tells us that they did not always.

oo The back close vowel is similar to the RP vowel, but used in different words.

yūĭ Westmorland seems to insert this diphthong where Cumberland and most Northern accents say "book". RP has another vowel in here, so "foot" and "strut" and "buck" and "book" do not rhyme in London.

oy is used in a few words in Westmorland, rarely and nearly always in words of French origin – "oil, choice, oyster". Wells at UCL classified vowels into 24 lexical sets. Each lexical set is named after a representative keyword. This one is the "choice" set.

These North Westmorland vowels are not exactly the same as Cumberland vowels. We would be interested to hear from readers who think they can identify all the phonemes in another accent of Cumbria. If your dialect sounds the initial "h", try to find every vowel, including diphthongs, that can be inserted between "h" and "d" to form a new word.

Consonants are easier, in the sense that the phonemes vary hardly at all throughout the English-speaking world. This is opposite to the Romance languages: Catalan differs from Spanish mainly in its consonants. English initial "h" and final "g" are sometimes dropped, and some sounds are elided in rapid speech, but the number of words we can distinguish does not change. We can of course make many more sounds than 24, but they are heard as the same "word" with a different "accent". Think of the Cockney, Irish and American ways of pronouncing "butter": the "t" is very different, but we still hear it as "butter". The table shows the systematic way of describing English RP consonants using IPA symbols. Most of the symbols can be read with their English sounds, except for those in the post-alveolar column. Six sounds involve stopping the air, then releasing it explosively, so these sounds are called either stops or plosives. Three phonemes allow some of the air to come out of the nose, and are called nasals. Eight sounds of English rely on friction as air rushes through a narrow gap, and are hence called fricatives. Two phonemes are part stop and part friction, so they are called affricates. The remaining four approximants involve the air squeezing between a narrow gap as the tongue gets near to, or "approximates" a nearby surface.

The consonants of Cumbrian English allow all the words of standard English to be distinguished, while for the following sounds the pronunciation is slightly different from RP.

h: it is well-known that that lower class speech drops the "h", so that elocutionists traditionally trained speakers of regional dialects to insert an "h", sometimes with the humorous results depicted in Pygmalion! in the south of Cumbria the dropping of the 'h' is common, so 'him' becomes 'im and 'how' becomes 'ow. In most of central and northern Cumbria the 'h' is normally retained; this is similar to Geordie speech in unusually retaining the "h" in lower-class speech. In fact h-insertion occurs in Cumbria: home is **hyam**.

l: The approximants "w" and "l" follow intriguing patterns. In parts of Cumbria, 'wall' becomes **waw**, 'pole' is **pow**. In phonetic terms, the "approximation" of the tongue to the palate here extends to include the lips. In 'wool' the "l" in final position and is deleted entirely, so the word is **woo**. Elsewhere the approximant "w" is inserted where RP does not have it: **yammly, wiet** and **fwoak** (in the Lance Porter extract above).

There is an interesting phonetic rule at work here, if we could only describe it!

r: Rollinson argues this "the Cumbrian 'r' is a flap, a very distinctive sound, and unique amongst the English counties; the tongue touches the roof of the mouth just once, producing a 'flapped' 'r' sound as in **threes** ('trees')" Most English accents have nearly lost the "r", so it is shown upside-down in the table; those that retain it often have rolled Scottish 'r'.

th: the alveolar stop "d' may be replaced by a soft 'th' (dental fricative), as in **wedder** (weather) and **fadder** (father); sometimes both sounds are there, as in "**wedther**".

Cumbria often retains Norse pronunciation where Standard English has "ch". 'Birch' is **birk** (ON björk), 'church' is **kirk**(ON *kirkja*), and 'chest' is **kist**(ON *kista*); however this is a preference for the West Norse word rather than replacement of the phoneme, so that "kip" and "chip" are still heard as two different words in Cumbrian. Similarly g (a velar stop) is used in **brig** ("bridge") where Standard English has a voiced affricate '-dge'. The West Norse accent has slowed the influence of London English. The place names **Keswick** and **Coniston** would have become "Chiswick" and "Kingston" by now, had they not been spoken with a Norse accent.

The glottal stop has not reached Cumberland! In many accents of English "t" and "d" are replaced by the glottal stop. In London this has progressed a long way, so that all six stops may be partly replaced by a glottal. There is no glottalisation in Cumbria, except in Barrow and West Cumberland, where people with different accents moved in for work.

Meaning and root	ON cognate	OE cognate
'draw', PIE *traghō	drag	draw
'make payment'	guild	yield
open, yawn PIE *ghanos	gape	yawn
chew at, gnagen, PIE *gnāmi	gnaw	nag
edge of sword, bird's egg	egg	edge
'to make muddy' PIE dher-	dregs	draught
cake	kaka	cécil (extinct)
place of worship	kirk	church
embankment	dike	ditch
earth to sit on	bank	bench
skyrta apron, ring-shirt etc.	skirt	shirt
ME schateren, N & S variants	scatter	shatter
'flay, divide' PIE *sken-	skin (OE hide)	sheath
bone with flesh cut off	skull, scalp	shell
loud cry	screech	shriek

scale, scant, scare, scarf, scathe, score, scrape, scrap, skate, skid, skill, skip, sky

When migrants from Angeln reached the British Isles around 450 CE, two sounds changed from Old Germanic: the /sk/ sound became /sh/, and the final /g/ became /y/. Danish remained "conservative" so the two ethnolinguistic groups were using the same lexicon with different sounds.

The English liked the Danish /sk/ sound and borrowed them again, so their "ships" acquired a "skipper". Practically all the 1,000 or so words starting with "sk" or sc" in modern English come from Danish. The table above shows some of the words.

Cumbrian has the stress features of its two source Germanic languages: initial stress followed by a variable number of unstressed syllables, by contrast with French equally-stressed syllables. The alliteration of both Beowulf and the sagas depend on repeating a start sound on the stressed syllables. There may be some persisting Norse morphology (ways of changing endings to make new functions. **Barnilaikins** is understood by some Cumbrians to mean "children's toys". It is not a simple addition of **barn**, noun for a child and the verb **laik,** as both elements are altered to

make the compound, more like Norwegian than English.

There is also an unusual breathing feature in Lakes and Icelandic. Most speech sounds involves an egressive air stream. Some Lakeland speakers also speak while breathing in, called an ingressive sound. In Danish, Swedish and Finnish the main function of inhaled speech seems to be paralinguistic, showing e.g., agreement with a statement and to encourage a speaker to continue. The majority of words that are subject to ingressive speech are feedback words (yes, no) or very short or primal (a cry of pain, sobbing). It also sometimes occurs in rapid counting, in order to maintain a steady air flow throughout a long series of unbroken sounds. In Icelandic whole phrases can be made ingressively.

In this chapter, we have tried to organise our stamp collection of Lakes language properly. There are several hundred whole words imported from West Norse, and a few from Welsh. We have outlined 19 vowels. Some big questions remain. What traces were left by the British women who first colonised Iceland? Is Cumberland more Cumbric than Westmorland? How did the Norsemen come to terms with the Saxons? We thank readers for their perseverance and invite readers to contribute childhood memories, linguistic analysis – or souvenirs from Iceland.

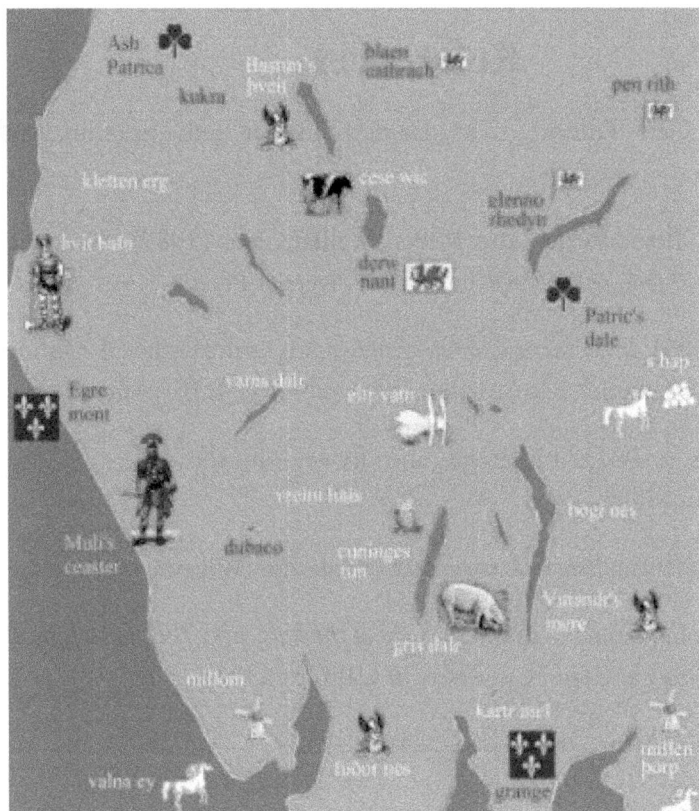

References

Anderson, Carl Edlund. "The Danish Tongue and Scandinavian Identity"

Andersson, Theodore M. and Miller, William Ian. (1989). *Law and Literature in Medieval Iceland* Stanford University Press

Baker, P.(2003). *Introduction to Old English*. Oxford: Blackwell. Online version at www.wmich.edu/medieval/research/rawl/IOE/pometer.html

Bradley,A.G. (1901). Highways and Byways in the Lake District. London: MacMillan.

Buntin,T.F. (1993). *Life in Langdale*. Kendal: Tom Wilson.

Byock, Jesse L. (trans.) (1990),*The Saga of the Volsungs: The Norse Epic of Sigurd the Dragon Slayer*. University of California Press

Byock, Jesse L. http://www.viking.ucla.edu/vita/

Callaway,E. (2015). UK mapped out by genetic ancestry. *Nature*. https://www.nature.com/articles/nature.2015.17136

Cameron,A. (1996). *Slate from Coniston*. Barrow-in-Furness: Cumbrian Amenity Trust Mining History Society.

Clark, John, and Yallop, Colin (1995). *An introduction to phonetics and phonology, 2nd. Edition*. Oxford: Blackwell.

Clunies Ross, Margaret (2010). *Cambridge Introduction to the Old Norse-Icelandic Saga*. Cambridge

Collingwood, William Gershom (1908). *Scandinavian Britain*. SPCK. Electronically copied by Project Runeberg

Cook. R. (trans.) (2006),*Njál's Saga*. Penguin.

Dickinson, William & Byers,R. (2006). *Comprehensive Dictionary of Cumberland Dialect. Cumbria*: Richard Byers. Reprinted from Dickinson, William (1859) Glossary of the Dialect of Cumberland .

E. Paul Durrenberger (1992). *The Dynamics of Medieval Iceland: Political Economy and Literature.* University of Iowa Press

Ekwall, Eilert (1936). *The concise Oxford dictionary of English place names.* Oxford: Clarendon Press.

Anthony Faulkes (trans.) (2001). *Three Icelandic Outlaw Sagas.* Everyman

Ferguson,R. (1873, 1998). *The dialect of Cumberland.* Llanerch Publications.

Field, John (1972). *English field names.* Newton Abbott: David and Charles

Gibson,A.C. (1873). *The Folk-speech of Cumberland and some districts adjacent.* Various publishers.

Goodacre, Helgason et al (2005). *Genetic evidence for a family-based Scandinavian settlement of Shetland and Orkney during the Viking periods.* http://www.nature.com/hdy/journal/v95/n2/full/6800661a.html

Helgason A, Siguradóttir A, Gulcher J, Ward R, Stefánsson K (2000b). *MtDNA and the origin of the Icelanders: deciphering signals of recent population history. Am J Hum Genet, 66: 999–1016.*

Helgason A, Nicholson G, Stefánsson K, Donnelly P (2003). *A reassessment of genetic diversity in Icelanders: strong evidence from multiple loci for relative homogeneity caused by genetic drift. Ann Hum Gen* 67: 281–297.

Icelandic saga database. http://sagadb.org/egils_saga

International Phonetic Association (2003). *Handbook of the International Phonetic Association: a guide to the use of the International Phonetic Alphabet.* Cambridge University Press.

Jespersen, O. (1946). *Modern English grammar on historical principles, Vol. 5.* London: George Allen and Unwin.

Karlsson, Gunnar (2000). *The History of Iceland.* University of Minnesota Press.

Kirkby,B. (1898). *Lakeland words.* Kendal: T.Wilson.

Ladefoged, Peter and Maddieson, Ian. (1996). *The sounds of the world's languages.* London: Blackwell.

Lakeland Dialect Society web-site: http://www.lakelanddialectsociety.org

Lee, Joan (1998). *The place names of Cumbria.* Manchester Free Press.

Manning, Jack. *South Cumbrian coastal dialect.*

Nicolson,J. and Burn,R. (1777). *The history and antiquities of Westmoreland and Cumberland.* London, 2 vols.

Opie, Peter and Iona (1960). *The lore and language of schoolchildren.* Oxford.

Relph.T. (2005). Lakeland Dialect. Journal of the Lakeland Dialect Society.

Rollinson, William (1997). *The Cumbrian Dictionary of Dialect, Tradition and Folklore*. Otley: Dalesman Publishing Co Ltd.

Rydland,K.(1982). Vowel differences and accent areas in Westmorland and North Lonsdale. Journal of the Lakeland Dialect Society.

Scandinavian Britain. Online at http://runeberg.org/scanbrit

Smiley, Jane (trans.) (2005). *The Sagas of Icelanders*. Penguin

Townend, Matthew (2009). *The Vikings and Victorian Lakeland: The Norse Medievalism of W. G. Collingwood and His Contemporaries*. Cumberland and Westmorland Antiquarian and Archaeological Society

Sweet, Henry (1882). *Anglo-Saxon Primer*. Revised by Norman Davis (1952). Oxford University Press.

Wawn, Andrew (2002) *The Vikings and the Victorians: Inventing the Old North in 19th-Century* Britain Brewer

Whaley, Diana (2002) (trans.), *Sagas of Warrior-Poets* Penguin.

Wells, John (1982). *Accents of English, vols I – III*. Cambridge: University Press.

Wright, Joe (ed) (1898-1905). *English dialect dictionary. Vols. 1 – 6*. London: H.Frowde.

Wright, Peter (1979). Cumbrian Dialect. Clapham: Dalesman Books.

Glossary

These are words of Scandinavian origin to be found in the dialect speech of Cumbria. The language abbreviation is the nearest connection between the Cumbrian word and a similar Scandinavian word. Abbreviations: Icel. Icelandic; D. Danish, N. Norwegian, OE. Old English, ON Old Norse, S. Swedish.

It is not a precise etymology, but shows a similarity at some historical point. We acknowledge The Cumbrian Dictionary of Dialect, Tradition and Folklore (W. Rollinson,1997) and The Dialect of Cumberland (Robert Ferguson 1873). The umlaut accent has its normal Germanic effect, e.g "ö" = oer; the circumflex (e.g. "å") is taken without change from Rollinson.

aback behind (ON âback - behind)

addle to earn (ON ödlaz - to obtain or acquire)

agate on the road (ON gata - road or way)

akin related (Icel. kyn - race)

anenst opposite to, against (ON giegnt - opposite)

angry painful or inflamed (Icel. angr - pain)

arklarge wooden chest (Icel. örk , OE aerc - chest

arrscar scratch, mark (Icel. ör = a scar)

arval refreshments given at a funeral (Icel. arfleifð - inheritance

arval breada small bun made from best wheat flour given to each mourner; arval cheese and arval ale also featured on these occasions

ask cold, a sharp wind (Icel. hastur - harsh)

assel-teeth molars (Icel. jaxl - molar)

atter spider (Icel. eitur, OE atter - poison)

attercob a spider's web

attermitea family likeness (Icel. aettarmot - family likeness)

axle-teeth the grinders (ON jaxlar - molars)

aye always. In the Icelandic Landnamabok the burial mound of Torf-Einarr is described as ae graenn - evergreen. (Icel. ae - ever, always)

bainnear (Icel. beinn - straight, short).

bainest way means the shortest way (Icel. beinstr vegr - the shortest route)

balka beam or partition (ON biâlki (beam, bâlkr (partition)

bang to strike, beat, surpass (Icel. bang - hammering)

barn child (bairn in north of county) (Icel. N. D. S. barn - child)

beal lowing of cattle, the sound of crying (Icel. baula - the lowing of cattle)

beck stream (ON bekkr - a stream)

beet to stoke or feed a fire (Icel. baeta - to improve, mend, repair)

berrier old name for thresher (Icel. berja - to strike, hit, beat, thrash)

bid to invite to a gathering e.g. wedding or funeral (Icel. bjoða - to invite)

bield place of shelter (Icel. baeli - a den)

bigg six-rowed barley (Icel. bygg, N. bygg, D. byg)

biggina building (Icel. bygging)

birk birch tree (ON björk, OE beorc - birch tree)

blea blue (e.g. Blea Tarn, bleaberries) (Icel. blár - blue)

blain to become white, bleach (ON bleikna - to become white)

blake pale yellow (ON bleikr - pale, fair)

boose stall for a cow (Icel. bás - stall)

borrana cairn, heap of stone (ON biarg - hill, heap)

brandling a small trout, also little worms used for fishing (ON branda - little trout)

brandreth iron tripod placed over a hearth for cooking (Icel. brandreið - a grate)

brant steep (Icel. brattur - steep)

bray to beat (ON braka - to beat, subdue)

brig bridge (ON bryggja)

camstop stones on a drystone wall (Icel. kambur - a ledge of rock. a combe)

carra flat marshy hollow (ON kjarr - a marshy place)

choop rose-hip, fruit of the dog rose (N kjupa - hip)

clag stick, adhere (D. kleog - sticky)

clap to pat or fondle (Icel. klappa - pat or stroke)

claver to climb, or cling to (ON klifra - to clamber)

cleg horsefly (Icel. kleggi - horse fly)

clemmed starved, parched (D. klemme - to starve; Icel. klemma - to pinch)

con squirrel (ON ikorni - squirrel) Place name Ickenthwaite is derived from this word.

coppy-steàl low wooden stool (N kubbe stol – a small stool from a log)

coup,cowp to upset, overturn (ON kippa - to tip over, upset)

cringle curved; e.g. Crinkle Crags circle Great Langdale (Icel. kringla - a circle)

cronk the cry of the raven (ON krunk - the cry of the raven)

crowdy oatmeal mixed with broth (ON grautr - porridge made from meal and water)

cush! cush! a call note for cattle (ON küs! küs! - similary used)

cushiepet name for a cow (Icel. kusa, ON kussa - used in the same way)

dadder to shake, tremble (ON datta - to vibrate; titra - to shiver)

daggy drizzly (Icel. ON deigr - moist with reference to weather)

dale valley (ON dalr - valley)

dalesmen inhabitants of a valley (Icel dala-menn - same meaning)

darrack a day's work (ON dagverk - a day's work)

deeve deafen (ON deyfa - to deafen, stun, stupify)

deg to dampen, sprinkle water on (Icel. döggva; ON doegva - to moisten)

dess to build up a pile (ON des - a rick)

donk moist, damp, dank (D dönke - to moisten)

donna the devil, or worthless person (Dan. dogenigt - a good-for nothing person)

dook to bathe, dive or stoop (Dan. dukke - to dibe, duck under the water)

dottle a small portion of tobacco left in a pipe, a small lump (Dan. dot - a stopper, ON ditta - to stop, close)

dowly melancholy, dismal, lonely (Icel. dauflegur - lonely, sad)

draff brewers grains (ON draf - dregs)

dree slow, tedious, dreary (D droi - tedious ON driûgr-gengginn - taking long to pass - in a road

drucken drunk (ON druckinn - Dan. drukken - drunk)

duffy soft spongy, woolly (ON tog - the rougher part of the fleece from toga, to draw out. Hence duffy is from the same root as tough which replaces the g sound with an f sound.

dub pool or deep water in a beck (Icel. djúpur - deep)

dump to butt with the horns (ON dumpa, Dan. dumpe - to strike, thump)

dwallow to wither, turn yellow with age (ON dvali - dullness, stupefaction, decay)

dwine to wither, pine away (ON dvina - to wither)

efter after (ON eftir - after)

elding fuel, firewood (Icel. ON eldur - fire)

ellers alder trees (Icel elri - alder trees)

esh the ash (ON eski - ash tree)

fain pleased, glad (Icel. feginn - pleased, glad)

fantickles freckles on the face (ON fina freckles+ tickle a slight mark)

feal to hide (ON fela - to hide)

feckless helpless, inefficient (ON feck - imperfect)

fell 1 mountain or high hill (Icel. N. S. fjell - mountain)

fell 2 to knock down with a blow (ON fella - to knock down)

fettle to fit, to mend (Icel. fella [pron. fettla] - to put in order)

firtle to trifle, to pretend to work (ON fitla - to fidget with the fingers)

flacker to flap or flutter (ON flaka - to flap)

flay to frighten (ON flaja - to put to fright) flaysome -something frightening

fleer to laugh (Dan flire - top smile sneeringly; N. flir - suppressed laughter)

flickflitch of bacon (Icel. flikki)

flipe brim of a hat (Icel. flipa - a flap)

flit to remove e.g. doing a moonleet flit (Icel. ON flyta - to move; N flyting - removal)

fluke flounder, flat fish (ON flôki - a flat fish)

foisty smell of damp and mould (ON fisa - to break wind)

force waterfall (Icel., N. foss - waterfall)

forelders ancestors, parents (Icel. foreldri - ancestor)

forset to waylay (ON forsât - to ambush)

fozzy soft and spongy as frosted turnips (ON fauskr - a rotten dry log)

frosk frog (ON froskr)

fudderment warm wrappings or lining (ON fôdr - lining)

galt male pig (ON galti, Icel. göltur - a boar)

gangrel a tramp, vagabond (ON gangleri - wanderer)

gar to compel, make to do (ON gera, giora - to make to do)

garn yarn (Icel. garn - yarn)

garth enclosure e.g. stack-garth (Icel. garður - an enclosure)

gate thoroughfare, road e.g. Clappersgate (Icel. N. gata - road, way)

gaum gumption, shrewdness, sense (Icel. gaumur - heed, attention)

gaumless lacking in sense

gavelock an iron crowbar (ON gaflok - a javelin)

gawp to gape, to stare (ON gapa - to stare)

gear dress, equipment (ON görvi - gear, apparel)

geldert snare made of horse hair for catching small birds (ON gilder - a snare; Icel. gildra - a trap)

getter one who begets (ON getara - one who gives birth to)

gezzlins goslings (Icel. gaeslingur - goslings)

gill ravine also spelt ghyll (ON gill - a ravine, deep gully)

gilt a sow pig that has had no young (ON gyltr, Icel. gilta - a young sow)

gimmer female sheep that has not borne a lamb under two years old (Icel. N. gimbr - a young female sheep)

giss!a call for swine (ON gris - a little pig)

glisky bright, sparkling often used of weather (ON glyssa - sparkle)

gloppened astonished, amazed (Icel. glupnaðr; ON glupna - astonished)

glower to stare, gaze intently (ON glôra - to stare like a cat)

goller to shout, holler (ON gaula - to bellow)

gomeral braggart, bully, cowardly person (Icel gambra - to boast)

goodlike handsome, good-looking (ON godlikr - good, virtuous)

gowk 1cuckoo (Icel. On gaukur - cuckoo)

gowk 2 a simpleton (ON gaukr - awkward)

gowk 3 the core of an apple (AS geolca - yolk as of an egg)

grave to dig (Icel. grafa OE grafan - to dig)

grime soot, smut (ON grîma - a black spot on the face) formally a mask or hood covering the face.

grimin' a sprinkling, slight covering of snow.

gripe a dung fork (Dan. greb - a stable fork)

gris, grise swine, young pigs (Icel. gris D gris - a young pig)

growpe a gutter behind the cows in a byre (ON grof Swe. grop - channel)

grun ground (ON grunnr - ground)

gryke a crevice in a hill side, or rocks (ON kryki - corner, recess)

haaf net net with a poke used for fishing esp. on Solway (Icel haf - the sea)

hadder drizzle, fine snow (ON hialldra - a thin snow shower)

hag to chop (ON hiacka - to chop, hack) hag-clog - a chopping block.

hag worm common snake or adder (Icel. höggormur - snake or serpent)

haistera surfeit (ON hasa - to have a surfeit of food)

handsel bargain, refers to exchange of money (Icel. hadsöl - the transference of a right, bargain, by shaking of hands ON handsala - a bargain)

hankle to entangle, to knot (Icel. hanka - to fasten, to knot)

hap, happins cover, wrap; bed covers (ON hjûpr, sheet, hypja - coarse covering

hartree the strongest post of a gate on which it swings (ON hiara - hinge)

harp on keep dwelling on a subject (ON harpa - to keep finding fault)

haver oats (Icel. hafrar - oats)

hesp door sneck (Icel. hespa - catch for a door)

hiding a beating (ON hida - to beat)

hirple hurkle, hocker To crouch, to stoop, to walk lame (Icel hokra, ON hurka - to crouch, ON hörkla - to hobble)

ing meadow (N ing - a field, meadow)

ishokles icicles (N isjökel - icicle)

jannock just, proper, fair (ON jafn - even or straight; or possibly Welsh iawn)

kave to move restlessly (ON kafa - spread, turn over hay, kava to fidget and move things

kebby-stick a hooked stick (ON kêppr - a stick, staff)

keld well or spring (Icel. ON kelda - a spring)

ken to know, be acquainted with (ON kenna)

kep catch (ON kippa - to snatch)

keowl a small piece of wood to measure mesh when making nets (Icel. kefla - a round stick)

keslop rennet, for curdling milk (Icel. kaesir - rennet and hlaup - coagulated milk)

ket carrion, offal, filth (Icel. ket, kjöt - flesh)

kevel to kick about (ON klaufi - awkward, clumsy)

kile boil, abscess (Icel. kyli - a boil or abscess)

kirk church (Icel. kirkja, N kirke)

kist chest for storage (Icel. ON kista - a chest)

kite the belly (ON kvidr - stomach)

kittle to tickle (Icel. kitla - to tickle)

kittling kitten (Icel. kettlingur, ON kettling - a kitten)

kye cows (ON kir - cows)

kysty fastidious, picky (Icel. kveistinn - fastidious, peevish)

laal, lile little (N. D. lille - little, small)

lafter brood of chickens (Icel. latr - the place where animals lay their young)

laik to play games (Icel. ON leika - to play)

laikin a child's toy (Icel. laikfang - a toy)

lait to search for (Icel. leita - to seek)

lambast to beat soundly (Icel. ON lemja - top thrash, to beat)

land-louper one who decamps without paying debts (ON land-hlaupari - a vagabond)

lang long (Icel. langur, OE lang - long)

langel, lanket a fetter for sheep, hobble (D. lænke - to fetter)

longsome tedious, weary (ON langsâmr - tedious

lathe barn, store (Icel. hlaöa, ON hlatha - a barn)

lave the rest (ON leifar - remainder)

laverock skylark (Icel. laevirki, ON laevirke - the lark)

lav-lug't having the ears hanging instead of erect (ON laf-eyrdr - hanging ears from lafa to hang)

lester, lister fish spear (Icel. ljöster - a salmon spear; N lyster - a fish spear)

ley scythe (Icel. ljár, N lja - a scythe)

lig to lie down, to lay (Icel. leggja, to lay, place, put)

limber supple, pliant (ON limpiaz - to become relaxed and slack)

limmers pair of cart shafts (ON limar - branches)

ling heather (ON ling - heather, any small shrub)

lisk groin (ON lysk)

lobscouse type of stew of meat and potatoes (N lapskaus - a stew)

loft a garret (ON lopt - a garret or top room)

lop flea (ON hloppa - a flea)

lound calm, sheltered, tranquil (Icel. logn - calm)

loup to leap or jump (ON hlaupa, OE hleapan - to leap)

low flame, blaze (Icel. logi - flame)

lowse loose, free (ON laus - free, released)

lug to drag or pull (N lugge - to pull by the hair)

lug ear; as in lug-marks - ownership marks in ears of animals (ON lög meaning law, possibly)

maa seagull (Icel. mávur - a seagull)

mawk maggot (Icel. maðkur, ON mathkr - maggot, worm)

mazed bewildered stupefied (ON masa - to jabber, N. masat - to fall asleep)

mazlin a simpleton from same source as mazed.

meal of milk the quantity of milk a cow gives at one milking (ON mâl, D. maal - measure)

meldur quantity of grain ground at one time (Icel. meldur - meal)

melgreaves quicksands (ON melr - a place full of sand)

mense politeness, decorum (ON mennskr - decency, order)

mickle much, great (ON mikill - same meaning)

middin a dunghill (ON mod - refuse and dyngia - heap)

middin-sump pool that received drainage from a middin (ON sub, D. sump - mire, bog)

mind to remember to take care (Icel. minna - to remind)

mirk dark, dusk (Icel. myrkur - darkness, gloom)

mowdiwarp the mole (Icel. moldvarpa, N moldvarp - the mole) from mold - earth and varpa to throw

muggy damp, thick, applied to weather (ON mugga - damp thick weather)

mull to crumble (ON mylia - to bruise or pulverise)

mun 1 mouth (Icel. munnur - mouth)

mun 2 must(ON mun, Icel. mun - must)

mush dust or powdery refuse (ON mosk N. musk - powder, dust)

nab to seize, to lay hold of (ON hnefa, D. nappa - to snatch)

naggy quarrelsome, contradictious (ON nagga - to rub, to chafe)

naggel to gnaw (Icel. naga - to gnaw)

neaf,neave fist (Icel. hnefi, ON nefi, OE neve - a fist)

neuk nook, corner (D. noff - an angle or corner)

nop to crop to nip ends off berries etc. (ON nappa - to pluck)

oo wool (ON ull - wool)

paddock toad (Icel. padda, N padde - a toad)

pash a heavy sudden downpour (D piaske - to splash)

pick to lift or throw (ON pikka - to cast)

pissimire an ant (ON maur, D. myre - ant - the prefix refers to the urinous smell)

poke,pooak cone-shaped bag, pouch or sack (Icel. poki - a bag)

pot skar fragment of broken pottery (N potteskar - pot-shard)

prod a thorn, sharp point (ON broddr - point or spike)

proddle to poke or prick - see above.

quern a hand mill for grinding corn (ON quörn - a hand mill)

quilt to beat (ON quelia - to kill)

quit free (Icel. kvittr - free)

quittance receipt (Icel. kvittun - a receipt)

raise a cairn of stones e.g Dunmail Raise (ON reisa - to raise)

rake narrow path along which sheep are driven (Icel. reka - to drive); to rake to wander aimlessly

rammish rank, pungent, sharp (Icel. rammur - bitter, pungent)

ratch to roam about roughly, rummage for something (ON reiki - a scent hound)

recklin weakest of a litter (ON reklingur - outcast)

reeans, reins strips of uncultivated land (ON rein - a grassy strip around arable land)

reek smoke (Icel. reykja - smoke) e.g. Reykjavik

render to melt tallow (ON renna - to flow, make liquid)

reuve to tear off (ON hranfa - to pluck, tear asunder)

rigg a ridge, log narrow hill (ON hryggr - the back, highest point on land or roof)

rise brushwood, copse wood (Icel. hris - brushwood)

rive to split or tear (Icel. rifa, N. rive - to tear, split)

ross horse (Icel. hross - a horse or mare) e.g. Rossthwaite

rootle to grub in the ground like a pig (D. rode - to grub as a pig or mole)

rowk mist in valleys (ON rakr - fog or mist)

rud-stake a pole that cattle were tied to (ON rud-staurr - cattle stake)

rung a staff or step on a ladder or gate (ON raung - rib of a boat)

sackless useless, helpless (Icel. saklaus - simple, innocent)

sark a shirt (Icel. serkur, OE serce - shirt)

scale to spread manure on a field (ON skilja - to separate)

scar cliff, bare rock (Icel. sker - a rock)

scarn cow dung (ON skarn - dung)

scoggers stockings with the feet cut off worn on the arms (ON skockr - sheath)

sconse seat in a recess (Icel. skonsa - a nook in a house)

scraak, skrike screech (Icel. skraekja, N skrike - to shriek)

scraffel to struggle, scramble (ON skreflas - to keep one's feet with difficulty)

scree debris of loose stones (ON skrida - to slip or slide)

scrogs stunted bushes, low brushwood (D. skrav - a twisted stunted branch)

scun to throw or hurl something (Icel. skunda - to speed, to rush)

scuta short tail e.g. that of a rabbit (ON skuts - a tail)

seeves, sieves rushes (Icel. sef, N. siv - a rush)

segs hard skin on palms of hands or soles of feet (Icel. sigg - thick, hard skin)

shaff! an expression of contempt (ON skraf - babbling, ranting)

shear to reap (ON skêra - to cut)

shillies shingle (ON skêlla - to clink, clatter as loose pebbles)

shive a slice of bread (ON skîfa - aslice)

sike a watercourse (Icel. siki - a small stream)

sime straw rope (Icel. sima - a rope or cord)

skarn dung (Icel. skarn - manure, dung)

skep circular basket made of rushes or straw beehive (ON skeppa - a basket)

skelp to smack, strike with open hand (ON skelfa - to strike with hand)

sken to squint (ON skå, D. skele - to squint)

skift to shift, remove (ON skipta, D. skifte - to shift or remove from one place to another)

skill knowledge (ON skil, skilja - to understand)

sladder to spill liquid (ON slagga - to spill, overflow)

slape slippery (Icel. sleipur - slippery)

slattery showery wet weather (ON sletta - to bespatter)

slaver to let saliva run from the mouth (ON slafra - to lick, N sleve - slaver)

sleck quench to extinguish (ON slöekva - to extinguish, D. slukke - to quench thirst)

sled sledge (ON sledi - D. slæde - a sledge)

slemp sly (ON sleyma - a scamp)

slipe to abscond (ON sleppa - to escape)

slobber to weep noisily (ON slurpa, D. slubre - to sup in a noisy way)

smit to smear or mark as with sheep (Icel. smyrja, OE smittan - to smear or anoint)

smittal infectious (N smittsom - contagious)

smoot the run of a hare or other animal through a fence or wall (N smau - a narrow passage; ON, Icel. smuga - a hole)

snerp to shrivel (D. snerpe - to tighten, contract)

snig to lop branches of fallen timber (N. snicka - to cut, work with a knife)

snod level, smooth (ON snoddin, N snöyydd - smooth, bare)

sonsy plump, voluptuous (D. sandselig - sensual, voluptuous)

soople the upper part of a flail (ON sveifla - to swing round)

spean to wean lambs etc. (Icel. speni - animal teat)

speer enquire (ON spyria - to investigate)

spelk small splinter of wood (Icel. spelkur - a shaving of wood)

spreckelt speckled (ON sprekklôttr)

stag a colt (ON staggr - the male of various wild animals)

stang a cart shaft (Icel. stöng, N stang - a post or pole)

steck to be obstinate, refuse to co-operate (ON steigr - stubborn)

stee ladder (Icel. stigi - a ladder, stigur - a steep path)

steg a gander (ON steggi - a male bird)

stiddy anvil (Icel. steðji - an anvil)

stoop a gatepost (ON stôlpi- D. stolpe - a post or pillar)

swath rind of bacon (ON svardr - skin of bacon)

sweel to burn unsteadily, to flare up (Icel. svaela - heat with thick smoke)

sye a drop small quantity of water oozing (ON sîe - to filter, strain)

syke a wet ditch or drain (ON siki - a watercourse)

syle to strain through a sieve e.g. milk (N. sila - to strain)

syme a straw rope (ON simi, D. sime - cord or rope)

taggy-bell curfew bell - (D. tække - to cover)

taistrel a worthless or disorderly person (ON teistr - a violent person

tak efter to resemble (ON taka eftir - imitate)

tak up to cease to rain (ON nû tekr ofan af - take up, become fine)

tarn a small lake (ON tjörn - a tear)

teem to pour out (Icel. taema - to empty)

teen lathe tithe barn (D. tiende - tenth, lathe - barn, Icel. hlaöa, ON hlatha - a barn)

thek, thak thatch (Icel. thak - thatch)

thick to be in league with (Icel. thekkja - to know, be acquainted with)

thivel a wooden stick for stirring esp. porridge (ON theyvel - porridge stick)

thoft seat in a boat (Icel. thófta - an oarsman's seat in a boat)

thole to endure, suffer (ON thola - to suffer, bear, endure)

thrang busy, occupied (ON thraungr - tight compressed, crowded)

threavetwenty four sheaves (D trave - a score of sheaves)

threep to dispute loudly, argue (ON threfa OE threapian - to argue, grumble)

throddyplump, well-thriven (ON thrutna - to swell, become round and plump)

thrunter, thrinter a three year old sheep (Icel. threvetur - three years old)

thwaite clearing (ON tviet - a piece of land that has been enclosed)

tike dog, also applied to an odd person (ON tik - a bitch)

till to 'Ista gaan till t' market?' (Icel. til - to)

toft the site of a deserted house (ON tômr - empty, N tomt - place where a house has stood)

toppin a curl of hair over the forehead (ON toppr - forelock)

traily slovenly (ON treglegr - slow, lazy)

tramp to travel on foot (ON trampa - to tread, stamp with foot)

trig tight, well-fitted (ON tryggia - to make secure, tryggr - safe, secure)

trod track or beaten way, footpath (ON trodd - a track or path)

tummelt to tumble or fall (N tumle - tumble, topple)

twinter two year old sheep has seen two winters (cf thrunter)

upto lift up (ON yppa - to elevate)

us short for house e.g. hoggus, peatus etc - from Scandinavian hus for house.

waits night musicians who played around Christmas (ON vakta - to watch, or keep awake)

wark ache e.g. heedwark, teethwark etc. (Icel. verkur - an ache)

watha ford (ON vad - a ford, a place that can be waded through)

welt to incline, to turn over on one side (Icel. velta - to roll over)

whick, wick living, alive (N kvikk - lively)

whisht! hush, silence! (ON hviska - to whisper)

whyea heifer of any age up to three years may also be spelt quey but pronounced with the 'wh' sound (Icel. kviga, ON quiga, D. quie - a heifer). The letter Q does not appear commonly in the dialect of Lakeland, and tends to be avoided by interchanging it with 'wh' for instance: quiet - **whiet**, quick - whick, squirt - whirt.

wizzent dried up, withered (ON visna - to wither, dry up)

wursle, russle wrestle (ON russla - to wrestle)

yan, yen one (ON einn - one)

yak oak (Icel. N eik - oak)

yal ale (ON öl - ale)

yam, hyam home (N heim - home)

yower, yewer udder of an animal (Icel. jugur, N jur - udder)

yule-log usually burned at Christmas from N. jôl - yule)